PLEASE

POPULATING THE PAST
Penmaenmawr's Mysterious Beginnings

POPULATING THE PAST

Penmaenmawr's Mysterious Beginnings

by Alwyn S. Evans

ISBN: 0-86381-880-3

Cover design: Sian Parri

First published in 2004 by
Gwasg Carreg Gwalch, 12 Iard yr Orsaf, Llanrwst,
Wales LL26 0EH
☎ 01492 642031   🖷 01492 641502
✆ books@carreg-gwalch.co.uk   website: www.carreg-gwalch.co.uk

Contents

Introduction

It has been my intention in this history to try to preserve what is left of the memory of a mountain which at one time was famed throughout Britain. It wasn't always remembered for the same reason and it meant different things to different people. In its way it has played a very significant part in the development of the village at its foot. Many Penmaenmawr families owe their very existence to the mountain, as without it their great grandfathers, grandfathers and fathers, husbands and brothers could not have made a living.

As a child I played on its slopes and walked through the quarry works with my father. Later, in adulthood I spent hours wandering over the moorland behind the disappearing quarry summit. Evidence of habitation, of religions and of human activity was all around; not all of the same period but spanning the years between the Stone Age and modern man.

Over the years I had read with great interest the fascinating accounts by the late, incomparable, Mr Ivor E. Davies, whom I knew as a family friend when I was much younger. With his wonderful newspaper articles he recreated in minute detail the buildings, families and characters of old Penmaenmawr.

Still I thought there was something missing. Some years later it dawned on me that what was overlooked was the fact that nothing, so far as I knew, had been written to illustrate the lives and times of those early inhabitants of Penmaenmawr.

I will not pretend that this brief history covers in detail the history of Penmaenmawr: that was never the intention. My purpose has been to attempt to put in some sort of order the events that have taken place on the hills behind the village. Ancient man, barely understood religions, invasions, slavery, poets, frightened travellers, aircraft crashes, quarrying, these are but some of the stages in its history and are themselves only the pickings of a far more complicated story. The mountain has seen the clearance of trees from its lower slopes as the climate changed and man decided that life there was to be preferred to the bleak existence on the windy and rain swept uplands. The summit of Braich-y-Dinas has been quarried away. In order to create his future, man has obliterated his past.

Perhaps this attempt at reconstructing that distant past will help future generations to appreciate how long 'Pen' has been here and how it began. The very fact that this history could be attempted is due to the foresight of a handful of scholars and local men who foresaw the loss of an irreplaceable slice of the past and had the courage and determination to do something about it. Their painstaking and detailed work carried out over several years between the early years of the century and the three or four years following the First World War has proved indispensable. It should be pointed out that these excavations were undertaken, sometimes in extreme, often in difficult and always in uncomfortable conditions of weather and altitude.

Where absolute fact is not known, no attempt has been made to romanticise, although several options, feasible and arguably otherwise have been included in the discussion. Any opinions presented are those of past historians or of learned bodies who have been involved in the discovery and study of ancient artefacts found around the Graiglwyd and Braich-y-Dinas area: they have not been altered or misrepresented in any way. Where the author's opinions have been put forward they have been identified as such.

My attempts at illustrating the lifestyles of the different ages are based on many years of interest and study in this field. Where evidence of life or habitation no longer exists because of quarrying activity, reconstruction of huts etc. is based on the measurements, finds and comments about the site recorded in the relevant excavation reports combined with the proven knowledge of similar hutments of the same period in other, similar sites.

Alwyn S. Evans

The Rise and Fall

It has been there since the dawn of time. Long before humans walked upright, the great bulk of Penmaenmawr dominated the northern coast of Wales between Conwy and Bangor: a distinctive landmark, visible for many miles. The mountain has been home to and has cast its shadow over many generations: from the Ice Age to the Computer Age its slopes have been occupied and worked, from summit to sea's edge.

Modern times

A brief overview

The late eighteenth and nineteenth centuries brought unexpected prosperity to many rural areas, provided indirectly by the birth of the French republic. After 1789 the once popular 'Grand Tours' of Europe undertaken by the wealthy had been made too hazardous by the French Revolution, the Napoleonic wars and the resultant military and social unrest on the continent: an alternative was urgently sought.

Wales and Scotland, until then considered rather boring and primitive backwaters, suddenly blossomed. Artists and poets had for years sought inspiration in their wild places and extolled their virtues to a largely apathetic public: now that public became the travelling classes and they clambered to see for themselves what had caused the artistic community to wax lyrical. The newly improved roads and developing railways brought previously remote areas within relatively easy reach. The industrial areas of the midlands and the Northwest of England and even the sedate Home Counties were only hours rather than days away.

Dwygyfylchi, as Penmaenmawr was more usually referred to at the time, was one such 'remote area' and the 'Grand Tourists' flooded in. The mountain, its name translates as 'Great Rock Head,' with its summit intact overlooked all. Its high moorland walks and the sea at its foot attracted the professional and the famous. Prime Minister Gladstone was a devotee and

Elgar the composer, seeking escape from his clashing imperial music came to relax in its peace and rural isolation. Families fleeing the depressing and debilitating effects of the smog and soot of urban life drank in the curative and bracing mix of sea and mountain air.

In the nineteenth century sea bathing had become a 'fad' and the tiny hamlet with its grand sweep of safe sand became famous as a kind of mini spa: at first, almost exclusively for the higher echelons of Victorian and Edwardian society. In 1861 Dr Norton built his Penmaenmawr Hotel overlooking the beach. A designer built spa hotel, it was provided with salt water bathing facilities both hot and cold. The water was driven up from a steam driven pump on the high water line. In keeping with the enthusiastic expansion of the time the name of the hotel was soon afterward changed to The Grand Hotel. Later, two world wars would prove to be great social levellers and the little resort with its modest apartments and solidly impressive boarding houses became a firm favourite with ordinary families who returned year after year.

Boom

Penmaenmawr had a further, less idyllic attraction; it was the nationally recognised producer of the hardest granite in the kingdom. Since the early nineteenth century the great hill's quarries had provided a livelihood for many of the families living in the village named after it. From its water streaked cliff faces too was hewn the stone to build the grand boarding houses and hotels to accommodate the well-heeled visitors. The iron hard setts or small blocks, chipped to shape by hand, resisted the iron shod wheels of carts and coaches without blemish. As the outside world became aware of the qualities of the stone, demand for it grew and the village attracted people for a different, more mercenary reason.

The developing quarry became a honey pot, attracting labour from within and without Wales. The village began to grow. The continuing inward migration of quarry workers and their families took the permanent population of Penmaenmawr from 826 in eighteen fifty-one to 3403 in nineteen hundred. From a tiny, self supporting farming and herring fishing hamlet at the turn of the eighteenth century, Pen' had exploded into a burgeoning, chapel building quarry village which doubled as a rather sedate holiday resort.

This was an unusual combination but strangely the destruction being wreaked upon the hillside did not appear to detract from the village's popularity. On the contrary, the small ships, first sailers and later coal and oil burners, which came to take away the stone, proved to be an added attraction on the sea front.

Decline

It was inevitable however that the quarry would eventually share the fate of nearly all other labour intensive industries. Technical advances in the quarrying industry resulted in the immense workforce of the late eighteen hundreds and the first half of the twentieth century being drastically reduced. Shortly before the First World War the records show that 1,082 men tore 517,000 tons of stone from the two quarries, Graiglwyd and Penmaen. Today, some forty men and their machines produce over 900,000 tonnes from the bowels of Penmaen alone and the visitors, grand and not so grand, have migrated like summer birds to destinations with more predictable weather.

The tide of holiday makers may have receded and the quarry work force declined; the population of the village on the other hand, although it has expanded slightly, has neither grown nor depleted significantly since the mid nineteen forties.

The villagers of today are less and less dependent on the

quarry. The days are gone when just about every family in Pen' had at least some connection with it. As a result people seem to have lost the intimate contact that they once had with the mountain and its surrounding ridges. Ask someone under sixty today where Fox Bank was and it is unlikely that they would know it from the high street Bank. They would probably be equally as unaware of places that rejoiced in names such as Yr Attic, Pen Marian, Kimberley, Bonc Jolly, Brake Bach, Y Gloch / Bell Yard, Pen Coed or Braich Llwyd. These and many others were household names a few decades ago but sadly no more. The whole thing has now come to be known, rather colourlessly, as 'The Quarry'.

'The Mountain,' on the other hand is popularly considered to be that relatively unspoiled part to the east of Ffridd Graiglwyd: beginning at Cwm Graiglwyd and including Moel Lus and the moorland behind which still attracts many walkers. It remains a convenient and attractive gateway to the Carneddau range.

Today the industrial face of Penmaenmawr has been cleaned up considerably. Commendable effort and no little expense has resulted in attractive change. The slopes of waste have been landscaped and re introduced trees, after years of struggle, have finally established themselves. It wasn't always so.

For most of the older inhabitants, and those brought up in its shadow during the nineteen thirties, forties and fifties, recollections of the quarry will undoubtedly be of ugliness and devastation, of heaps of chippings and cement-like waste, of unsightly and dilapidated buildings and busy railway inclines.

At the foot of the mountain, where the expressway now runs and just to the west of the railway station there was a small marshalling yard popularly known as 'The sidings'. This was always full of row upon row of wagons, filled to the brim with granite chippings, being constantly nudged and clanked into the correct order for despatch to the towns and cities of Northwest England and beyond. On the beach, two loading jetties ran out into the sea and small coasters took the produce of the quarry to a hundred destinations, at 500 to 1100 tons a time. In Britain and on the continent, streets, avenues and stately boulevards were made of Pen' 'setts': railways ran on lines embedded in Penmaenmawr ballast and the crushed stone was used in concrete for a thousand construction enterprises.

Without a doubt though, for those living in the villages of Llanfairfechan and perhaps particularly Penmaenmawr, the most enduring though not endearing memory of the quarry's heyday is of dust. The fine grey dust was the inevitable result of the activity in the stone crushing mills and was carried up on open conveyor belts to the constantly patrolling breeze. As the wind regularly changed direction, the dust spread and impartially laid a grey white coat on the dwellings of great and humble alike. It could find a line of washing or a polished windowsill with unerring accuracy within a radius of two miles around the quarry and penetrated even the most skilfully sealed house.

A fresh look

Although this work is not intended to be a description of the quarry and its workings, in any writing about the Penmaenmawr uplands some mention of the industry is unavoidable. The old mountain and its quarry were vital to the village's prosperity. For so many years the great scars and heaps of waste have been Pen's most obvious features. To do full justice to the history of the Penmaenmawr quarries would require it to be done in isolation. It would be an undertaking that also required an intimate knowledge of the industry, which I do not possess.

Neither is this meant to be a 'village history' as such. The histories of the parish of Dwygyfylchi and the villages or 'districts' of Pant-yr-Afon, Capelulo and Penmaenan have been covered many times and in many forms. This is an attempt to take a fresh look at one part of the ridge that dominates Penmaenmawr and to try to unravel some of its history, which culminated in the fateful decision to reduce its majesty by removing its crown. Hopefully too it will answer some of the questions that have been asked over the years and are still asked from time to time regarding some of the developments which took place before the creation of the village and the coming of the quarry.

The questions

At some time many of us have asked, or are likely to have been asked, 'Where was the axe factory?', 'I've heard they made stone axes, but I don't know where', 'Is there anything to see?', 'There was a fort on the top wasn't there?' 'Yes, The Romans built it', or 'Yes, it was a Stone Age fort', or 'I've heard there was but I think it's only a rumour!' Even, 'I've lived here all my life, I've never heard of it'.

People, particularly newcomers to the village continue to ask questions about the rumour they've heard of the fort on the summit. The nebulous fort and its inhabitants must surely rank as one of the most important yet least explained pieces of Penmaenmawr's history. Although it is almost always referred to in isolation, it must have been connected to the surrounding plateau and its overall evolution. With this in mind, I hope to present as full a picture as the incomplete evidence will allow.

The ridge

Since the beginning of recorded time, this relatively short shoulder of high ground, some one and a half miles long by a little over half a mile wide has featured in the development of Penmaenmawr. (Fig. 1) During those years it has been host to a variety of peoples and ventures. It has seen primitive stone chippers, priesthood, Invasion, civil war, international war, struggling farmers and hardy quarrymen: and almost as soon as the wheel was invented the great bulk became the bane of travellers attempting to negotiate the precipices at its foot in order to pass along the coastal strip.

Apart from the excavations on Braich-y-Dinas, which form an integral part of the account, the story makes little reference to modern times. It is important therefore that if it is to make sense, this reconstruction must be undertaken in a reasonably

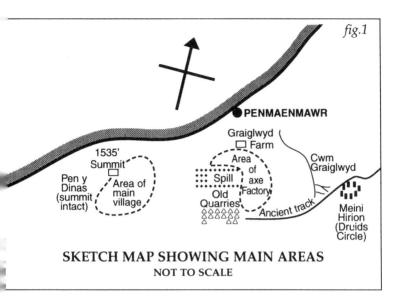

SKETCH MAP SHOWING MAIN AREAS
NOT TO SCALE

correct historical sequence and a convenient chronological order

The tale spans the period between c. 3500 BC and about 400 AD. Several different peoples and three main periods in history are involved in its telling. The new or late Stone Age, the Bronze Age and the Iron Age. To aid continuation, that part which deals with the Iron Age has been extended to involve the Roman occupation up to and including its decline. When we talk of such 'ages', care is needed to avoid drawing a line between each period as if one came neatly to an end one day and the next period began on the following day, month or week. The evolution from the Neolithic to the copper and bronze ages for example, took place over hundreds upon hundreds, even thousands of years. During that time, periods overlapped and overtook each other so that some places and peoples were still in a 'Stone' age while others were further developed. It must not be thought for example that simply because iron was discovered in one area or country, bronze was discarded everywhere else. Bronze might have been superseded by iron but it remained in general use alongside iron until the seventeenth century and for some, more specialist purposes, it is still in use today.

A convenient place to start is what is considered to be the point where the first human activity on the slopes can be safely recognised: the stone axe 'factory' on Ffridd Graiglwyd. Continuing a short distance to the South, the history will take in The Druid's circle before turning West to deal with the peak of Braich-y-Dinas. The word Dinas translates as City and Pen is Head or summit. The suggestion is then that this was the peak or head of the city. It will be seen as the clues come to light, that in our case city might perhaps be a little generous; village or fortified village would be more appropriate. An element of misunderstanding can occur when Dinas is translated as fort, as sometimes happens.

Where hard evidence has been found to exist on and under the ground, providing this mental reproduction has been relatively uncomplicated. Where actual site evidence is lacking, use has been made of documented history of other, similar locations to illuminate those at Penmaenmawr. The picture becomes a little clearer when dealing with the summit and its fort or village. Considerably more physical and documentary evidence is available following the excavations on that site than on the others. Much more has been unearthed to provide dates of occupation and so on.

The axe factory for instance, despite examination, preserves most of its secrets. The picture on the ffridd appears at first to be uncomplicated: people made axes there. When any attempt is made to put down basic building blocks though, the picture clouds over and becomes tantalisingly elusive and fragmented. The whole situation there has had to be reconstructed entirely from the items recovered and their recorded distribution. (Fig. 2)

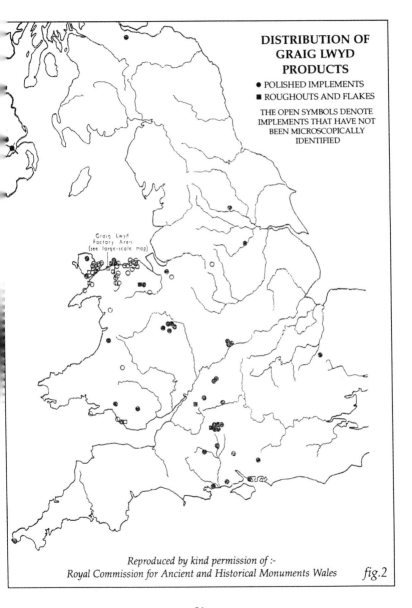

DISTRIBUTION OF GRAIG LWYD PRODUCTS

● POLISHED IMPLEMENTS

■ ROUGHOUTS AND FLAKES

THE OPEN SYMBOLS DENOTE IMPLEMENTS THAT HAVE NOT BEEN MICROSCOPICALLY IDENTIFIED

Graig Lwyd Factory Area (see large-scale map)

Reproduced by kind permission of :-
Royal Commission for Ancient and Historical Monuments Wales

fig.2

More detailed knowledge of similar sites elsewhere of the same era has provided some of the glue. The pieces have been put together, but who knows whether here and there, because of limited data, some of them might not be upside down or in the wrong places?

The enigma of the stones of Y Meini Hirion or Druids' Circle must also remain largely unsolved. Even though evidence was found at the site, such as it was was limited to funerary and associated activities: any clues to the original purpose of the stones were considered lost thousands of years ago. Like the many others of its kind spread around the British Isles, it remains part of an ancient, ephemeral world.

With regard to the people concerned in each of these sites: they can be identified only by the time in which they lived. The artefacts they left behind sometimes give us an insight into their life style. They therefore necessarily form part of a general illustration. Any attempt at more detailed identification such as tribal affiliation would undoubtedly result in extremely risky speculation.

In short, reconstructing what went on in such and such a place and when, is comparatively straight forward. It is when we try to identify with any degree of exactitude, the people who chipped the axes, erected the stone rings or built the fort or village that we suddenly find ourselves up against history's brick walls.

It will be realised that in attempting to tell this story some guesswork has been inevitable but where this is the case the possibilities are argued and the outcome put forward as reasoned speculation and not as provable fact. The full picture is that created by the considerable knowledge now available of the periods concerned. Where this could not be applied directly to the area in question, comparison with similar sites elsewhere has provided a firm base on which to work.

What follows then is the putting together of all this information, speculation, expert scholarly opinion, and where it is available, forensic evidence, in an attempt to give an insight into the ancient happenings along the ridge above Penmaenmawr.

The beginnings

Some 450,000,000 years ago a stream of molten magma pierced the earth's crust. This pushed up the surface, forming a monstrous hump. As it came into contact with the atmosphere it cooled and plugged the hole through which it had erupted. That volcanic surge and the different rates at which the lava cooled resulted in two very similar types of rock but with different properties. Those properties were to decide the course of the history of the hills and the resulting skyline.

For many millions of years this volcanic activity, known as an intrusion or Laccolith, lay hidden under several kilometres of shale and, during the ice ages, even a kilometre or two of ice as well.

Eventually, temperature change and many centuries of constant erosion of the surface revealed the hard, igneous rock that was to become Braich-y-Dinas and its surrounding ridges. Further movement and minor eruptions took place until finally the area settled down.

Time passed and the landscape went through a series of changes until it became a fairly benign environment that we might recognise today. Humankind had long since emerged as the dominant animal and was moulding the surrounding countryside to improve its lifestyle. Large tracts of forest were cleared and fields created. To achieve this, tools were needed and the skills to use them. The creation of these tools is the first step in our journey of investigation.

Graiglwyd Rock

It is difficult to ascertain how early the first primitive humans first found that certain stones could be chipped to form a sharp edge and where such stone was to be found. No sooner is one date arrived at than continuing research and another discovery confounds it. Archaeology has shown that Neanderthals and even Homo Erectus, two of the species that preceded Homo Sapiens or modern man, were creating sharpened stone chips several million years ago.

What *is* clear, is that once the discovery was made, in the years that followed, the process was perfected. It remained, with fire, arguably the most significant aspect of early man's development until the discovery of metals. The stone on Graiglwyd (1100 ft) proved to be ideal for the making of weapons, tools and domestic implements because it possessed those ultra hard, crystalline properties similar to flint, which made accurate shaping and fine edges possible. Known commonly as granite, the correct description for the rock chosen to make the implements is Augite Granophyre. Whereas the great volcanic intrusion that formed Pen-y-Dinas is Porphyritic Diabase, a hard and extremely durable stone, it was its great shoulder to the east to which ancient man was attracted.

Sites in Britain where other suitable stone was recognised became centres for the production and export of stone axes, scrapers, spear and arrowheads and so forth. Although some arrowheads and the odd skin scraper have been found, the main products at Graiglwyd appear to have been axes and axe heads. Picks and similarly shaped tools are thought to have been the result of the mineral properties and not the worker dictating the final shape of individual pieces of stone.

Of the three sites which made up the 'factory', two are above Llanfairfechan at map references SH 115 MR 698739 and SH 115

MR 691735. The third site, the most famous and easiest to visit, is on Ffridd Graiglwyd itself and lies at SH 115 MR 718754/5. It is this latter location which falls within the confines of this description. The total area involved at this site was a sweeping curve from a little way above Graiglwyd farm, upward to the eastern end of Clip-yr-Orsedd. Anyone planning to visit the site should be aware that there is no vehicular access and no *public* parking within at least a half mile of the site. Despite that, it can be reached quite easily by a steady walk without any hazards.

Many of the unfinished axes and the accompanying waste were found on the summit and upper slopes of the Graiglwyd pasture. The ridge surface here was already partially uncovered by natural erosion and conveniently lent itself to immediate exploitation. It would seem that the best rock, with the qualities required for ease and accuracy of flaking was found on the extremities of those outcrops. Years of weathering had shattered the rock and the resultant debris was already near the required size. As a result of this piece of luck, the amount of chipping and flaking would be greatly reduced. The ridge of live rock was also left exposed and cracked in such a way that breaking off of a suitable piece was not too difficult. The exposed section used to make the prime quality tools was completely quarried away by modern methods many years ago.

The actual making of the artefacts is not surrounded by any mystique. The technique of chipping and polishing of such tools had been recognised for years. The puzzle when dealing with Graiglwyd is not when or how but who?

Who were these people who inhabited the slopes and produced the axes? How many were there? Where did they live? These are the questions that spring to mind: unfortunately the answers do not: they remain unclear. During this chapter some attempts at identification are made although I fear the results are less than complete.

The outcome of several ad-hoc searches and finds, reports of planned and scientifically undertaken excavations and surveys, together with a choice of opinions and verdicts regarding the influx of various peoples to Britain will all be considered. The result is still not a clear, definite picture but a series of options open to a variety of interpretations. As already stated, what *will* become clear is that far more questions can be asked than answered.

The Axe Factory

The story of the Penmaenmawr Axe Factory begins for us, not, as one might imagine, on a bleak mountaintop at the dawn of history but on a fine summer's day in June 1919.

While on holiday in the district shortly after the First World War, Mr and Mrs S.H. Warren found themselves crunching across some obviously unnaturally uniformly shaped shale and paused to take a closer look. What they found was astonishing; it was the waste created by the constant chipping action used to fashion stone axes many centuries before.

Being an antiquarian by occupation and competent field observer and an archaeologist by inclination, Mr Hazzeldine Warren was swift to realise the importance of their find and took immediate steps to recover as much as possible of the existing evidence. He reported his discovery to the Geological Society and his first report on the site was published in the *Journal of the Royal Anthropological Institute* of the same year.

In order that any proposed excavation was undertaken in a systematic way, the Institute formed a committee to oversee the proceedings. Under the auspices of this committee, work to clear and explore the site began on the 21st of May 1920 and lasted for one month.

To enable the greatest amount of area to be covered and to hurry the process of clearing away brush and surface rubble, a gang of men was recruited and, supervised by Mr Hazzeldine Warren began exploring the site. They were apparently paid for by the committee formed earlier, part of whose duties was to raise funds for just such an event. A railway strike in 1919 meant that distribution and consequently production slowed at the quarries. If they were amongst those laid off as a result, the team hired by Warren would have been glad of the alternative employment.

On the 4th of June 1920, just a fortnight into the excavations, Hazzeldine Warren was so inspired that he sent a post card to Mr J.W. Jackson, keeper of the Manchester Museum proclaiming excitedly that 'we have got about 50 stone axes'. Unfortunately, his excitement at finding such a depository of Neolithic artefacts coupled no doubt with the constant fear that time and money would run out, led him to conduct the excavations in what would be regarded today as a less than professional way.

His approach to the task was reminiscent of that employed by Heinrich Schliemann in 1871 at Hissarlik the debated Turkish site of ancient Troy. Both men were somewhat cavalier in their approach and concentrated on finds rather than keeping records. Mr Hazzeldine Warren did however make accurate maps of the sites involved and left several accounts in different publications.

Many excavations of this type were conducted in those days without the care and precision that would be applied today with regard to the depth at which a find is made and its position relevant to other discoveries and so on. In the years since Graiglwyd was first explored techniques and technology have advanced beyond what those early enthusiasts would have considered possible. It would be quite wrong therefore to fault the methods that were used at Graiglwyd in 1920 from the safety of a computer desk more than 80 years after the event.

Three expeditions, each of approximately one month were undertaken through 1919 to 1922. Mr C.H. Darbishire financed the 1922 dig. This last assault on the slopes had a slightly humorous edge to it. Mr Ivor E. Davies, with the agreement of the quarry management, had organised a team of seven men from the quarry to help with the heavier work. Hazzeldine Warren in the mean time had been busily trying to raise financial aid for the expedition. Manchester Museum's ruling body sympathised with Hazzeldine Warren in his search for funds but did not grant money to the cause. Instead they sent Mr Jackson the keeper of the museum, accompanied by his wife to assist for some days in the actual process of digging. The couple arrived on the 16th of June and set up their headquarters in the Glyn Hotel Penmaenmawr. From there the couple took part in three of the four weeks allocated to the dig. Mr Jackson's reactions to his substitution in lieu of a financial grant are not recorded!

As a result of the team's efforts that year many broken and unfinished axes were discovered as well as an enormous amount of waste. Three tons of worked stone were collected altogether over the three seasons and this included over 1000 examples of axes at varying stages of manufacture. Despite the vast number of examples recovered only four fragments of finished, polished axes were found.

Although the area concerned was well known locally, it is difficult to say whether the full importance of the site was suspected. Mr R.D. Darbishire the quarry owner, a keen and competent amateur historian and other locals had made earlier, smaller discoveries but it was the find by Mr Hazzeldine Warren, which put Graiglwyd firmly on the archaeological map. It is now recognised as having been the third largest site in Britain when in production.

Mr Warren was a member of several Geologically associated bodies and it was in his capacity as representative of the Royal Anthropological Institute that he wrote to several of the London papers describing his discovery. It was not long before Mr Warren was invited to speak to a number of interested groups and he took full advantage of the opportunity to elaborate on the extent of his discovery and its importance. It can be seen from the hyperbole in the article reproduced below that Mr

Warren's understandable excitement and enthusiasm infected at least one major newspaper of the time.

Stone Axe Factory

Thousands of prehistoric weapons found

Mr S Hazzeldine Warren is to give a lecture in London upon his remarkable discovery of a vast Stone-axe factory which flourished on the slopes of a Welsh mountain between four and six thousand years ago.

This discovery made by Mr and Mrs Warren while walking over Penmaenmawr in the summer of 1919, has created enormous interest in scientific circles. A committee representing a number of societies has been formed to explore the site and distribute representative collections to the museums of this country and Europe.

It is hoped to discover specimens of stone implements made in this great prehistoric Birmingham or Sheffield in distant counties and even countries, for there is no doubt that the fame of great stone age factories travelled and tribes trekked hundreds of miles through the swamps and forests to make or buy implements they wanted.

Arriving at the scene, Mr Warren pictures the lighting of campfires, the preparation of the food killed and made ready with stone axes and knives, and the 'The music of the flakes' as the granite was split and fashioned into axes, adzes, chisels and other domestic implements.

Thousands of Specimens

During his investigation in 1919 and 1920 Mr Warren found literally thousands of stone axes in every stage of manufacture. Some were rough resembling the earlier flint work of the

Palaeolithic age: others were polished in the later Neolithic style.

'We found many axes finished but broken by a last blow,' said Mr Warren in an interview. 'We were able to put together 30 complete specimens of these, which we call our 'prehistoric d..n's. You can imagine the feeling if not the word used, when after hours if not days of patient work the prehistoric man ruined his work by an unlucky blow. We also found axes that had been roughly re-pointed and these we took to be implements brought to the spot and discarded when new axes had been fashioned.'

The chief scientific interest of this great discovery lies in the fact that the material used was a so-called 'granite' instead of flint. The extent of the factory is also remarkable, covering as it does hundreds of acres. There are traces of 'hearths' in the district, which may be the last remains of the dwellings of the axe makers. The nature and use made of the implements suggest that it flourished at a time of peace when prehistoric man was more interested in cutting and polishing wood for dwellings and boats than in making war weapons.

Techniques and working conditions

The technology involved in producing the implements was rudimentary and consisted of a suitably shaped stone being hammered and chipped using another stone of different qualities. The so-called Hammer Stones were often beach pebbles, rounded and smoothed by the action of the waves, or river pebbles with similar characteristics. The stones destined to become the axes were readily available in the piles of scree worn from the peaks by an eternity of fierce sea wind, hard frosts and driven, lashing rain. Sometimes flat stone 'anvils' were used on which to rest the axe while it was being fashioned.

Each family or group would occupy an area on which they intended to work. Known as 'hearths', these cleared and sometimes roughly paved patches of ground would cover an area of some 20ft by 15ft. A hearth found on Graiglwyd is described thus: 'The base was formed of selected stones three to five inches in diameter, covered by a good deal of charcoal, and many axes or flakes, more or less burnt.' The account goes on to describe how a great mass of flakes and broken roughouts lay on the down hill side, and round this hearth and a number of small hearths nearby were an accumulation of the small chips produced in the final trimming process. The debris connected with this hearth was considered to appear to belong to one period of working.

If the workers were to spend some time on the hillside, and the method of working suggests that they would: it follows that they would have built rude shelters to keep off the worst of the elements. Disappointingly, despite searches at the point of work and nearby, nowhere on Graiglwyd has definite evidence of such constructions come to light.

On and around these hearths the evidence of axe making could be found. Large scatterings of flakes and charcoal showed these to be the scenes of considerable activity. It is now generally agreed that the greater percentage of the roughs was formed here but ground and polished elsewhere: perhaps in a more benevolent environment lower down the slopes and nearer the home comforts of a village. It is known that some roughs for instance were carried as far as Llandygái and polished at the settlement there, while others were discovered near Abergele. (Fig. 3)

The number of samples found over the years and especially the great mass brought to light in 1919 confirms that there was a demand for these implements. We now know that there was a widespread distribution of the Graiglwyd implements, particularly around North Wales as might be expected but also down into the south of what is now modern England and North

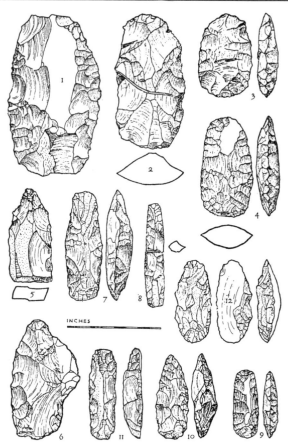

Graiglwyd, Caernarvonshire.
Selected types of Axes from the Factory.
Based on Hazzledine Warren.

Block loaned and reproduced by kind permission of:
The Director, National Museum of Wales

Reproduced by kind permission of:
Royal Commission for Ancient and Historical Monuments Wales   *fig.3*

to the Scottish borders. These more distant finds are usually single items and need not necessarily demonstrate an established trade route but simply the migration of one individual or the passing of such an item from hand to hand as the result of trade. The possibility of the existence of a more elaborate distribution has been mooted on several occasions however.

Distribution by land

A discussion about the means of large-scale distribution of the axes reveals some of the difficulties facing the toolmakers and puts forward a selection of the possibilities open to them. This is not intended to be regarded as cast iron proof of what happened in those distant times. It merely puts together some known facts and adapts them to the conditions facing a potential exporter of axes from Ffridd Graiglwyd.

During the Neolithic era in North Wales, the coastal areas were fairly heavily wooded and tracks were rare, difficult to negotiate and generally confined to the higher ground. Disposal of the axe factory products in any volume by land would have been difficult.

Animals could have been used to carry fairly sizeable loads but here there are problems. Horses were much smaller than those we might recognise. They would have been more accurately described as ponies, similar in size and form to the Dartmoor pony. It is likely also that they were rare and probably the property of chieftains or tribal leaders: in any case horses are not thought to have been widely domesticated until the advent of the 'Beaker People' some time after the highpoint of the Graiglwyd axe industry. Oxen were available but of course had to be obtained and had to be fed and sheltered. Their price and maintenance is likely to have put them beyond the means of our axe makers.

The beasts, had they been present, could have been employed to pull primitive carts, or a framework of poles similar to the North American Indian 'Travois'. Rough wooden sledges might have been built but all of these are likely to have been of such a rudimentary design and the surfaces, over which they would have travelled, so rough, that the contraptions would very soon have fallen apart. None of these forms of distribution can therefore be realistically considered as bulk transport.

One might ask. 'Couldn't they carry the axes themselves?' It would not have been impossible to deploy the axes in such a way but it would have proved impractical to carry any appreciable amount for more than a few miles. Anyone who has carried a small haversack containing a flask, a camera and a few sandwiches for several hours on mountain tracks can appreciate that it doesn't take long for even that small pack to have trebled its weight. We can safely assume then that the mental picture we might have of a man struggling uphill with a large sack of rocks on his back is probably a non-starter. There is little doubt that a small number of tools were passed on in such a fashion but mass distribution, if it ever took place, would not have been feasible using such methods. At this juncture it would be appropriate to add that whenever Graiglwyd axes are mentioned in articles or books about the production of stone axes, they are inevitably referred to as finds of single items or at most two or three at a time. Undoubtedly this has led to an unquestioning acceptance that the axes were only distributed in very small numbers or even as single items passed from hand to hand. Although this almost certainly took place, it is difficult to reconcile the widespread activity and the concerted effort over many hundreds of years on the slopes with the production of one or two tools or weapons at a time. The exploitation of such a site over such a long period must surely have been done with the satisfaction of a larger market in mind. The means of transport for such an enterprise *was* on hand: the sea, and beyond that, the rivers.

Water-borne commerce in the Celtic Sea and within the British Isles was surprisingly well developed in Neolithic times and known trade routes are shown in the diagram below. (Fig. 4) The stone roughs could have been transported to the beach by being physically carried during several journeys. They might also have been taken down on sledges of some form pulled by perhaps two men, one of whom might act as the 'brake man' on the more severe downward gradients and a commercially

fig.4

NEOLITHIC SEA TRAVEL WAS WELL DEVELOPED AND FAR REACHING

viable load put onto the primitive but seaworthy craft then available. This method, with the men being replaced by a horse but still using a brakeman was used in the early nineteenth century to carry rock to the beach to be used as ballast by passing ships. Perhaps two or three men carrying loads on their back down the relatively short distance to the sea might be more realistic.

Distribution by sea

The vessels of the time were dugout canoes made from whole tree trunks or slightly more sophisticated vessels made of tanned animal skins stretched tightly over a frame of stout Ash or Hazel rods. For the transport of such a heavy and sharp edged load, perhaps the hollowed log would likely have been safer: the hide boat being more suited for the carriage of people and soft goods such as skins and foodstuffs. The dugout or log boat should not be compared to a Red Indian canoe or suchlike: it could be of considerable size but with a surprisingly shallow draught.

Examples of such working boats of that period found in Britain have been as long as thirty-five feet though most would have been somewhat shorter. One or two examples of hulls recovered were made from more than one tree. They were about fifty feet in length and had a beam of about four feet. It is believed that a log boat of this length would not have proved suitable for sea voyages because of the anticipated instability of such a craft in any conditions more active than a gentle swell.

Large vessels were plying between Britain and the continent however. In 1963, Mr Wright, a fellow of the Royal Society of Antiquaries whose pet topic was ancient boats, came across some old timbers on the banks of the Humber estuary. Investigation revealed them to be the remnants of an ancient seagoing cargo vessel.

The ship was estimated to have been some fifty two feet in length with room for eighteen paddlers. There appeared to have been room for a mast but the existence of such a feature was not proved. The planks had been sewn together using pliable yew branches. The ship was dated to between 2030 BC and 1780 BC with a probable date of 1900 BC being accepted. This was not the first ship of this kind to be discovered; Mr Wright had found two others in the same area some years earlier. It is believed that the vessels were used to carry exceptional loads of unusual weight or size and not everyday commerce. The dating of such a ship puts it at the latter end of activities on Ffridd Graiglwyd and although unlikely to have been used in the activities here, it serves to portray a level of sophistication beyond the popular image of a heavily browed man sitting in a crudely carved log.

The average working boat of some twenty to twenty-five feet would have been of a thickness that varied from two inches at the sides to four inches at the bottom. It has been calculated that one such boat found in Poole in Dorset would have been capable of carrying approximately three thousand eight hundred pounds of cargo and four men in less than sixteen inches of water.

The sea level is known to have been lower in Neolithic times and this would have meant that the shoreline between say the mouth of the Ogwen river and the Conwy would have been broader, pierced by narrow shallow channels leading to the sea. The shorter log boats with their shallow draught were ideal for such conditions. Once loaded, the ballast effect of the rocks and the paddlers would have kept the vessels stable. Such log boat designs outlived the prehistoric period and survived into the fourteenth century, no doubt because of their phenomenal load carrying capacity, shallow draught and stability in coastal waters and rivers.

The boats would then sail to secondary distribution points where the axes could be finished and made available to population concentrations. Centres such as this have been identified at Prestatyn, Bournemouth and the Severn estuary. It is easy to see that once in the Severn Estuary for instance; the more densely populated Wessex and Salisbury plains would be brought within range.

This information regarding boats, sledges and so on is not meant to infer that such large scale operations went on in ancient Penmaenmawr but simply demonstrates the capabilities and possibilities of the age.

The people

Who were these Stone Age craftsmen? Can we identify them? Did they have a name? Have any remnants been found of their houses?

Questions like these have been asked over the years and no satisfactory answer has, so far as the writer knows, ever been decided upon. In trying to formulate answers we find more questions. It has been suggested that it was possible that these people were not resident at all, perhaps they were seasonal visitors to the North Wales sites from the more densely populated areas in the south of England. Modern archaeology does not start to apportion identity on a tribal basis to peoples in Britain until about 2,600 BC. Even then they are only usually recognised by their pottery or funerary rights and named accordingly; for example 'The Beaker People or the Mound People'. Before that date they tend to be referred to en masse as Neolithic or Mesolithic and so on. It is known that the activities on the Graiglwyd slopes took place over many years, possibly centuries, during the latter part of the stone ages and, arguably even into the Bronze. It is therefore relatively safe to refer to the artisans of Graiglwyd as Neolithic.

What is known of Neolithic people tells us that they were of slight build and sinewy and their skulls were inclined to be

40

longer and narrower than those of modern man. They dressed in a mixture of coarse woven material and primitively styled leather garments and wore laced wrap around leather sandals. The discovery and exploration of many similar sites of the same period has revealed that their garments although primitive, were shaped and fashioned to resemble clothing that we would recognise today. They were **not** the cartoon image of cave men who carried clubs and addressed each other as ugh!

We also know that the lives of Neolithic peoples were generally hard and the life span short. If they were fortunate enough to avoid falling victim to disease or violence, women could expect to live to thirty on average and men perhaps five years longer: a situation reversed as civilisation progressed! Excavation and forensic science has revealed that they were prone to arthritis and many have been identified as having had broken limbs, which were more often than not allowed to set naturally, often with crippling results. Infant mortality was frightening. Research has shown that even in reasonably 'advanced' culture centres in Britain fewer than half would survive infancy, 30% would die during childhood, 50% of those who survived died before reaching the age of 15. It would be safe to assume therefore that in the more hostile upland environment of north Wales the survival rate was likely to have been even worse.

Although the hunter-gatherer nomad still existed, in general a more settled way of life now prevailed. Crop growing and animal husbandry required scrub and forest clearance on a grand scale and made permanent farmsteads a feature of the landscape.

Their pottery was hand made without the aid of the wheel, by pressing rolled lengths of clay on top of each other. It was not fired properly, simply being allowed to dry naturally until it was stable and then buried under a heap of embers covered and sealed by turf or soil. The resultant vessel would not withstand prolonged exposure to naked flame. Forensic investigation has revealed that as a result, most of their meals probably consisted of a luke-warm gruel, made mainly of pulses or root vegetables with the occasional scrap of meat or fish and perhaps shellfish or the occasional wild fowl, which would have been plentiful on the wide expanse of swampy sea shore. These then were Penmaenmawr's first quarrymen. Ironically, the commercial value of the stone, which these primitive people recognised, was to lead to the eventual industrial rape of the mountain, its disfigurement and its eventual disembowelling.

Who were they?

If the people were indigenous then where were their huts or dwellings? As stated earlier there is no evidence *on the Ffridd* to support permanence. The remains of hut circles survive near the work area but as a result of study by Mr Hazzeldine Warren and his colleagues and others since, it has been decided that although they are ancient they are of a period much later than the activity at the axe factory. On the plateau above there are several hut platforms and a variety of clues suggesting permanent habitation: ancient, but not of the era in question. Several small hollows and valleys nearby could have provided sheltered places to build huts. If such shelters were erected then it is likely that they were of a 'lean to' type, framed with wood and walled where applicable with mud and wattle. The roofs would have been of rough thatch or turf or even tanned skins stretched between poles. All must have rotted away without trace for nothing has been found to suggest their existence.

It has been suggested too that these early entrepreneurs came to the Penmaenmawr hills on a seasonal basis: that they perhaps belonged to the tribes settled in what later became Wessex. That there was a fairly advanced culture developing in the South at that time is well established.

Some sources have gone so far as to state that the axe makers may have been those expert flint workers who mined for flint at Grimes graves and Cissbury in Norfolk. If so how did they arrive in Penmaenmawr, did they walk, bringing their families with them? The distance from Norfolk to north Wales is over two hundred miles: a fair journey today, unimaginable in 3000 BC. If they chose that route then how did they navigate? Could they instead have elected to sail from Norfolk along the coast each spring until they reached the northern shores of Wales? It would certainly have been possible to do so even with the limited technology of the time.

Although the actual journey was feasible, It would have been totally dependent upon the weather, which could have capsized them or kept them on shore for days or even weeks. Even in perfect conditions and covering at best no more than a few miles each day, is it likely that they would have struggled all that way? If that is what happened then it must have taken many months and perhaps even years, taking place only during the gentler months of spring and summer. With that in mind then we must consider that their intention must have been to settle permanently and not spend a limited time here, only to return with a few axes!

As they struggled along the south coast, why would they have ignored Cornwall, a granite peninsula, which was much nearer? Axes identified as having come from the Cornish sites have been found in the Salisbury area at such major sites as Windmill Hill, Avebury, Durrington Walls and so on. Was another group already using the Cornish area?

Did the visitors combine the work on Graiglwyd with trade at the great orme with its copper mines? Could they have been work teams from the copper mines whose job it was to make tools to help in the mining and the felling of trees for fuel and shelter?

Did they come, not from the South as is often surmised, but from settlements on the North East Coast where adventurous bands had been arriving over many years from what is now North Germany and Belgium?

In the autumn of 1926 the Reverend H.G.O. Kendall MA, a keen amateur historian and archaeologist, paid a visit to the Graiglwyd site. Together with his son and a small band of helpers he carried out his own inspection, which yielded little that had not been previously found. In his account of the search he studiously avoided the problem of who the axe makers were or where they came from.

Having arrived from whatever source, how did they sustain themselves? Did they bring food with them and if so how long would it have lasted? If they came from as far afield as Salisbury Plain did they stay long enough to sow crops? If they did, then allowing for tillage, sowing, growth and harvest, each visit must have lasted at least twelve months.

It seems likely that if their visits were short, say, several weeks, and the mode of work so time consuming, that they would have been reluctant to use up valuable time collecting wild food and hunting. Does that mean that they brought families with them? If so then it must be supposed that shelter, however temporary would have been erected. If children were involved they might have required milk animals: goats perhaps, or sheep?

The amount of logistical planning and inconvenience required to support a temporary stay, however short, must have been considerable and tends to lend weight to the argument that the workers were local residents: perhaps not on Graiglwyd itself but not too far away. Could it be that their home base was at Llandygái and that they came by boat along the coast? Perhaps they came overland from the settlements in the Conwy valley or at the mouth of the Ogwen, perhaps using the route which runs alongside Y Meini Hirion (Druids' Circle) high up on the ridge above. If they did choose such overland routes then the quantity of supply material they brought with them must have been even less than if they had come by sea.

Supposing they were indigenous: did they live in one of the dry stone encampments elsewhere on the hills? It is doubtless quite misleading to look at this through twentieth or twenty-first century eyes. Whereas we almost immediately put the elimination of inconvenience fairly high on our list of priorities, their prime consideration would have been survival. We are in the main loath to walk anywhere when we can ride, they, on the other hand would likely have thought little of rising before first light to walk to their place of production and returning at dusk. Assuming they could travel for two or three hours at perhaps two or three miles an hour on average, that could place them anywhere within a radius of between four and nine miles of Graiglwyd and its subsidiaries above Llanfairfechan. Perhaps they only stayed on site long enough to create a few roughs: maybe a day or two, or a week. Such short stays as opposed to the conjectured full summer occupation of the site might explain the paucity of dwellings.

In further support of the theory that they could have been local is the fact that it would have taken many years of constant practice, handed down from generation to generation, to be able to produce roughs of the correct size and shape. Sett making in more recent times was a similar art and was considered a specialist craft, attracting higher wages and taking many years to perfect, albeit with sharper, metal tools.

It remains unproven but it is within the realms of possibility that it was local tribesmen and not the Wessex tribes who carried the axes in rough boats to the centres of population: returning perhaps with high quality copper tools, some wheel turned clay pots and a few new ideas.

What *is* certain is that someone was here and they *did* chip out the rough shapes of axe heads and skin scrapers. The evidence for that is unchallengeable. All else remains speculation.

Further surveys and excavation of the Graiglwyd site were undertaken between 1992 and 1994. These were funded by the

Royal Commission for Ancient and Historical Monuments in Wales, The University of Wales Bangor, Cadw, the National Museum of Wales and the Gwynedd Archaeological trust. In the main they tended to confirm the finds and conclusions reached so many years before, although the field of exploration was widened to take in areas threatened by potential expansion of the quarry. Examples of the material found on Graiglwyd can be seen in The National Museum of Wales and representative collections are preserved in many other museums throughout the British Isles.

Y meini hirion (The long stones)

The Druids' Circle

Known locally as Druids' Circle this ring of stones is to be found on the ridge above Penmaenmawr at 1,300 ft at map ref. SH.722746. Today, ten stones can be described as still standing, some have fallen and yet others have been removed. The circle itself is 82 ft in diameter and stands directly within a rubble and earth bank now some 4ft wide and a little over 1ft high. At least one ancient account, if taken at face value, suggests that a dry stone 'wall' enclosed the circle, but no height is given. There is a recognisable entrance to the Western edge although unexplained blasting in the 19th century significantly damaged it. In his Tours in Wales, Thomas Pennant describes the site as having ten upright stones, the largest of which was 8ft 3ins; another stone lay on the ground. This one he measured at 11ft 2 ins. Both have long since disappeared and no doubt having been shortened and dressed now form the posts for someone's gate. This has been common practice throughout the highland regions of Britain wherever standing stones are to be found: they also make good animal scratching posts.

There appears to be some disagreement about the actual date of the circle. Aubrey Burl in his 'Rings of Stone' 1979 has the henge erected at some point between c. 2000 BC and c. 2200 BC. An excavation carried out by The Royal Commission for Ancient and Historical Monuments in 1958 came to the conclusion that 1300 to 1500 BC would be more likely.

Whichever date we accept, Penmaenmawr's circle can be considered to be fairly late in the calendar of Britain's circle and henge building phase. The first circles in Britain are known to have been put up around 3300 BC. The first henge at the Llandygái group, some eight or nine miles to the west was erected between 3200 BC and 2880 BC.

Although at first it appears to be standing in majestic isolation, The Druids' Circle is in fact the main example in a series of large and small circles and groups of stones covering a wide area. For the purposes of this work, only the main circle and one subsidiary will be discussed in detail.

The circle stands close by an early Bronze Age trade route, which is thought to predate it. The route can still be traced from Cors-y-Carneddau to the stone formations at Bryn Derwydd (Druid Hill), locally referred to as Red Farm; and from there, it is likely to have run into the Conwy valley or along the coast to other settlements.

Contrary to what the popular name suggests, the stone monument predates the druids by perhaps 600 to 1000 years. Although the orthodox mental picture associated with such stone circles is that created by the Victorian romantic movement, of old, white bearded men in long flowing robes invoking the gods and distributing secret potions: it is unlikely that anything of the sort took place at Penmaenmawr's henge. The druids in Britain are regarded as having been at the height of their power and prestige considerably later, from the first century BC to the first and second centuries AD. By then the original reasons for the erection of the circles were probably as much a mystery to the druids as the druids are to us.

Circles of this type have for centuries presented the problem of use. Many theories have been expounded over the years and the favourite appears to be that they were some kind of astrological calculator or calendar. Although that could reasonably be believed of intricately constructed henges such as Stonehenge or some of the Hebredean monuments, it is difficult to apply the same theory with any confidence to a rough circle of undressed stones like the one at Graiglwyd.

Keeping that in mind, it is interesting to consider that according to Professor Alexander Thom, this ring was planned as an ellipse based on two right angle triangles. Perhaps it is not so rough after all! He wrote, 'One of the almost perfect triangles . . . It would have been quite impossible for the builders to detect the discrepancy in the hypotenuse, from their point of view the perimeter was also perfect'. If so much care was taken when the stones were erected, then obviously the people who undertook the feat had some degree of mathematical knowledge and could apply it. But to what end? As the circle was put up at the latter end of the henge-building period, did the people who erected it do so while not fully understanding the ancient rituals and reasons?

Apparently not if we are to accept Dr Aubrey Burle's theory in 'The Stonehenge people'. Here he suggests that 'The probable reason for the non-circular shapes was to lay out a long axis that would act as an astronomical sightline. This was a method often used by builders of stone 'circles' at sites such as Cultoon on Islay, The Twelve Apostles near Dumfries and the Druids' Circle in North Wales.' Despite Dr Burle's explanation, the excavation plan produced by the Royal Commission of Ancient and Historical Monuments, Wales portrays the monument as being round with a *slight* elongation to the WNW. It could hardly be described as an alignment. (Fig. 5)

How?

Another question, which raises all sorts of difficulties, is the one of construction. For example, let us consider the size of some of the stones. Those standing today are a fair size and the records suggest that some in the past were considerably bigger. Where did they come from? Were they already conveniently on the spot?

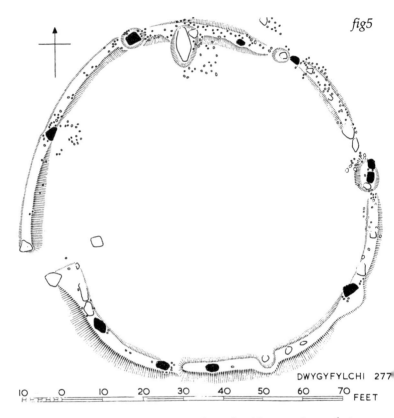

fig5

DWYGYFYLCHI 277

10   0   10   20   30   40   50   60   70 FEET

The moors thereabouts are dotted with a variety of stones, many of which could have been glacial deposits, already shaped by nature to be stood on end. We must assume that the stones forming the circle were dragged to that certain spot: if so, by whom and how? The ground behind that area today is usually quite boggy, it is soft even in the summer: if it were the same then, it would have made the act of dragging the stones to their allotted places extremely difficult.

Sir John Wynne of Gwydir (1553-1627) gives a brief insight into conditions during the late sixteenth century. In an account of the area he says 'This place is fyne delicate dry pasture, and hath beene aunciently inclosed and inhabited, as appereth by the foundacions of stone wales which are everywhere to be discerned, and by the ridges which are in many places soe apparent as yf itt had beene plowed within this six yeeres.'

With Sir John's words in mind, let us consider that the work might have been undertaken in the dry months and that the ground was conveniently stable. Some of the bigger stones were said to have stood eight or more feet above ground. With at least three feet in the ground to keep them stable, they would have been about ten to twelve feet long and with a girth of some eight to ten feet. Dragging such a huge stone over unprepared ground, even for a short distance would seem an unlikely option. Alternatively, how many people, using the technology of the time would have been required to lever a stone of those proportions onto a series of logs or even a sledge in order to transport it?

Even if the stones were conveniently close and the chosen mode of transport functioned successfully, the manpower required would have been considerable. They then had to erect the stones in their respective holes: presumably under the direction of some kind of local shaman who, according to many renowned historians would have demanded accuracy of positioning. How long would the work have taken?

The reason I put forward this series of problems is that the population in the immediate area was arguably sparse, their lives governed by the seasons and whose cereal crops and animals were vital to their existence. Could they have afforded to allocate so much of their time and manpower to the erection of a circle of stones like Y Meini Hirion? If yes, then perhaps the population was greater than imagined and the reasons most compelling.

Perhaps their priests told them that the erection of such a monument was essential to the production of their crops. If as is sometimes supposed, the circle provided the seasonal information needed to time the planting, then perhaps it *was* essential. Perhaps I have been dismissive of their expertise, was it a calendar after all? The reason, what ever it was, must have been considered absolutely vital for them to devote so much of their important time to fulfilling it.

Let us assume then that the population was big enough to be able to spare some able bodied members for this sort of work. How many would they have been, twenty, fifty? If we were to decide on fifty and that team represented let's says fifty per cent of the available manpower, then we are talking about a group of villages or individual huts sufficient to house a hundred men, without taking into consideration the women and children. Where did they live?

Other than the nearby fort, which is considered to be of a much later date, why is there no trace of a settlement large enough to have supported them? There are lots of small hut groups scattered over the hills and moors in the vicinity, indeed one such settlement and evidence of a field system lies only a couple of hundred yards away on Clip-yr-Orsedd, but no large central village complex such as those found in lowland areas. A little short of a mile away, on the southern slopes of Tal-y-Fan there are several small settlements, each housing one or perhaps two families. It would take many such groups to provide a construction team large enough to erect the circle and still leave enough of a workforce to tend the cattle and the fields.

Could it be that some small groups of men, maybe four or five, nominated by their tribe or group to undertake the work, were not necessarily local but travelled considerable distances to stay on the spot and labour for an allotted period with others from nearby groups. If one takes into consideration all the small settlements and defences in the lower Conwy valley and westward down the coast there was a considerable pool of manpower available which, if well organised, could have completed such a task.

By using such a system, a sizeable workforce could have been formed without denuding any one village of too large a proportion of its manpower. It is likely then, if that is how it happened, that a central body must have organised such an endeavour. Was there a presiding hierarchy of chieftains or holymen who would have wielded such power? If so, where did *they* live? Within the fortifications on Pen-y-Dinas?

How long would it have taken? The first henge at Llandygái was begun at about 3200 BC: the final stage was completed at about the same time as the Druids' circle was put up, about 1300 to 15000 BC. Stonehenge, from stage 1 to stage 111c took 1300 years to complete. Admittedly Penmaenmawr's circle is not in that league but it does serve to put things in perspective.

Bones, teeth, druids and astrology

As time slipped by the original purpose of the stones became distorted and eventually lost. Were the people who erected them displaced by a different, perhaps more warlike race? It has been considered that the Neolithic axe flakers were either displaced or assimilated into a race with broader, more rounded skulls whose lifestyle was superior to those of the earlier inhabitants. These newcomers with their higher skill levels were undoubtedly responsible for the henges: using them for specific though still unidentified purposes. It could be that these were of a religious nature, certainly they had some sacred significance, as later excavations were to show.

Children

In 1958, Mr W.E Griffiths of the Royal Commission for Ancient Monuments undertook an excavation, which exposed one Cist burial of cremated bones and two secondary burials, again of crushed bones but without Cist walls. The evidence suggested that the first was a child of 10 or 11 and one of the others the burial of the cremated and crushed bones of a child between 11 and 13. At the third cremation all that could be deduced was that there had been a cremation. There was nothing in any of the burials to indicate the sex of the children. The ages were arrived at with such precision because two teeth and a small piece of jawbone with a tooth cavity had survived relatively intact. The cavity was too small to have accommodated an adult tooth. It was surmised therefore that the child was younger than thirteen, apparently the age at which adult teeth reach their final size. The surviving teeth were later than milk teeth so therefore they were presumed to have belonged to a child over ten years of age.

All the remains had been contained in rough clay food jars. This form of burial is known as urn burial and is useful in that the food vessels concerned can be fairly safely dated. The remains of one child were in a vessel with corded 'maggot' impressions. These markings and decorations were made by twisting short lengths of clay into a maggot shape and pressing them onto the vessel, hence the name. They were rarely used as decoration after c. 1400 BC and would imply therefore that the burial took place during the early part of the circle's life. The containers were then interred in stone cists made of flat slabs. The Cist in Druids' Circle faces North to South. This was a favoured form of burial of The Beaker people. Their worship was sun orientated rather than the moon orientated religion of the earlier Neolithic. The corpses were laid with the head to the south, men faced to the east and women to the west. It has been suggested that if buried North to South and lying on their right side, the male dead would be 'reborn' with the rising sun each day. It is difficult to see why women should have been faced the opposite way. In the case of the Penmaenmawr ring, the cist itself lay north to South but the remains were cremated and interred in a clay jar with no specific alignment.

The second pit was found a short distance from the centre of the circle and contained the remains of another young child. The urn in this case was not decorated. Smooth undecorated vessels were a feature of later times and this together with the off centre positioning might suggest a later burial or the burial of a child of lesser station. A third burial, again off centre, was so decayed as to be virtually worthless from a recognition standpoint. With the children, were found a small bronze knife, a roughed out axe head of 'Graiglwyd' origin, some flint scrapers and flakes and a scattering of quartz stones.

One of the pits had a short and shallow trench leading from it to a wide hole lined with whetstones. It is Professor Aubrey Burl's opinion that the whet stones and other artefacts buried with the children were probably votive offerings. This does not automatically mean however that the children were sacrificed here or that they were sacrificed at all.

Nothing could be discerned of the nature of the childrens' deaths because of the intensity of the crushing of the bones and the corrosive damage suffered as a result of the acidic nature of the surrounding soil and peat. It was impossible to tell whether they were sacrifices or the victims of disease or accident.

At a time in man's history when every surviving child was another pair of working hands, common sense suggests that it is unlikely to have been the former and is far more likely to have been sickness, which claimed them. This however is reasoning from a modern standpoint. It would be wise to consider what professor Aubrey Burl had to say on the matter.

'At what may be the most dreadful of all the megalithic rings, the Druids' circle overlooking Conwy Bay, there is other evidence. The ring has a stark and splendid setting alongside an old trackway. The thirty stones once stood in a bank of boulders and rubble, broken by an entrance at the Southwest emphasised by cumbrous portal stones. Today the interior is empty and quiet, the grass blown by the ceaseless moorland wind, but under it there lay a cist where quartz stones had been dropped.

In the cist there lay the cremated bones of a child. Near it was a pit holding the remains of another child. A third child cremation was found nearby. It would be remarkable if these were simply burials of children, isolated from parents and other adults, laid to rest at the centre of an important ritual circle, and as one looks down on the Druids' circle from a ridge of hard rock one wonders what rites had been performed inside it.'

Part of a poem by R.D. Ray also requires some contemplation.

It shows how easy it would be to be led by our imaginations, to recreate the Victorian pan-Celticism and accept without question that these rings were the venue for sinister acts.

High above I stand
In a bitter, bleak blown land,
Ragged with rocks crag cruel,
Under the buzzard's wing
Of yore,
With grim grappling they reared
This wind worn rain-racked ring,
Of late
Someone, digging, found
A drift of white pebbles,
A bronze knife
And childrens' fire charred bones.

Although the immediate reaction to the finding of bones would be to assume that the rings were burial places, one has to ask, why only three children? We assume that as a place of worship, it must have been active for many years perhaps several centuries. Only three children in all that time? Was it a burial place at the same time that it was a place of worship? Was the first child a sacrifice and the others simply the later burials of a superstitious hill folk? If so, how did they know where to bury the children unless the original grave was marked in some way or it was recent enough for them to know where it was?

Did the sacrifices and burials coincide with some astrological event, which occurred every so many years, perhaps hundreds of years? That might account for the small number and the off centre position of the secondary graves where the ceremony was repeated. If that *were* the case, how would the people concerned have known when to make their sacrifices? If the first sacrifice was made early in the circle's life, did the people concerned in the later events still have a pre druidical shaman sect, which retained sufficiently accurate mathematical and astrological expertise to give a precise date? If the happenings took place at a much later date, were the druids involved: if they were, were they using the same circle but making the sacrifices for a totally different reason?

Why not adults?

It could be argued that as the ring is situated so close to an ancient trading track, perhaps the children, apart from the main cist grave, were from different family or tribal groups and died elsewhere, and at different times, of some illness. They could then have been cremated and their bones crushed. When the family group travelled on a trade journey, which they knew would bring them along this track, did they transport the ashes and bones here to be buried in what was considered to be a religious sanctuary? If that is the case, and bearing in mind the monument's position near a track which must have been used by hundreds of people from many different families over the centuries, why not others, why only three?

In those times the chances of surviving child hood were slim. There must have been many others. Why weren't they buried here? Could these three have been of rank? Were they brought here after death to be cremated and buried within the circle, or was at least one of them killed here in order to appease the gods when the ring was completed? If so, one wonders how he or she was chosen and what their response was when they realised what was about to happen! If sacrifice did take place, was the victim first sedated and if so with what?

Woodhenge in Wiltshire has within the main circle three smaller rings. In one of these the body of a child of three or four was found. The skull had been cleft in two, and not after death. It is difficult beyond imagination for the modern mind to grasp such a deed and the grief of the parents. Even though the child might have been chosen as an honour, I doubt the mother would see it in such a light.

A few feet to the West of the Druids' Circle are the remains of a ring-cairn. The cremated bones of a young woman were found here, together with some evidence of charcoal and some patches of burnt ground. Again the question arises, Why only one? Rank or position perhaps? The monument had been there for many centuries. Why in all that time was only one young female considered sufficiently worthy to be buried within it? Many similar rings are to be found all over Britain and some, though not many, share the kind of evidence found at Druids' circle; the cremation and burial of children, never more than one or two, together with quartz stones and small votive offerings.

Many of these rings occupy positions similar to the Penmaenmawr circle: high, remote places often with little to invite habitation. All are devoid of any evidence that they could have been places of work. They have nothing to indicate that they were inhabited, nothing to contradict the belief that they were purely and simply places of worship or sacred ceremony.

As the centuries passed, odd stories and superstitions grew around the eerie stones and one or two relating to the Druids' Circle are retold here. There is one stone in the circle that is called the deity stone. It will bend toward and strike anyone who uses bad language in its presence. Another stone, with a shallow hollow on its top is called the Sacrifice stone. Rumour had it that if a child were placed in the hollow during the first month of life; it would have luck forever. This latter is also said of immersion of a child or its clothing in the well at Llangelynnin old church.

As time went by and the original uses for the rings were forgotten; would it not be logical to assume that other, secular uses would have evolved? Later peoples, unaware of the purposes of the circles might not have treated them with the respect and reverence their origins demanded. Certainly, later folk did not, as they dragged them away to make gate posts and support walls and so on.

Positioned as they were on the trade track, it is not beyond the bounds of possibility that they could have been used as a meeting point for travellers or itinerant tradesmen. What an ideal venue they would have provided for the conducting of business, the sale of cattle and sheep. Marriage ceremonies could well have been performed within the circle, or the blessing of babies. Is it possible that those unfortunate children and the young lady buried within the circles were the deceased young and a wife or daughter of the earlier leaders of the nearby fort who buried them there without really understanding the stones' true purpose? The list of possibilities is as long as the imagination.

In the late sixteenth century, Sir John Wynne of Gwedir (*Gwydir*) gave his opinion of the stones and what they might have stood for. The spelling is that of the reign of Charles the 1st and has not been altered in any way.

Sir John Wynne's account:

'Aboutes a myle from this ffortiffication standeth the rarest monument that is to bee found in all Snodwden, called Y Meini Hirion; ytt standes within the p'ishe of Dwygyfylchi, above Twdduglasse, (*Gwddw Glas, Green Gorge*), uppon the playne mountaygne. This monumto (*monument*) standes round as a

59

circle, compassed about with a stone walle:and within the walle, close under the walle, are long greate stones round about the circle, standynge uppon there endes in the grounde, that a man would wonder where in these partes such stones weare to be found, and howe they weare soe sett uppon there endes in the ground. Ther are of these stones now standynge in this circle, as I take it, twelve; whereof some of them are two yards and three quarters, some two yardes some a yarde and three quarters above ground, besydes what is within the ground. The circle within these large stones, which wee call Meini Hirion is every way in breadth some six and twenty yardes; this standes uppon the playne mountaygne as soon as you come to the height, and hath much playne even ground about ytt. Ytt should seem that this was a place whereunto the ayncient Bryttaynes came from the dinas aforesayd to encampe themsealves and trayne there souldiers; ytt stands in a plane ffitte for justes and tournamentes and this circle thus rounded with these long stones might bee the place where the kinge's tente was pitched, and neer to this circle are three pretty big stones uppon their andes standynge triangle-wiese, lieke a tribbet (tripod?), whereuppon as they say was sett a great cauldron to boyle meal in, and surely those three stones doe look as if they had been longe in a great ffyre.

Some two or three flightes shoots (*Distance of an arrow shot, each flighte perhaps some one hundred and fifty to two hundred yards. author*) from this place are diverse greate heapes of small stones, which wee call carneddi. And in this place there was a greate battayle fought between the Romans and the Bryttaynes, where the Romans were overthrowne and a greate slaughter of both sydes. And such as were slayne weare buried in heapes one uppon another, and these stones caste uppon them least the wild bores and swyne shoulde digge upp there bodies.'

Sir John was of course adapting the area to suit the activities of his day such as the jousting but we must not dismiss his ideas out of hand. A ridge nearby and to the seaward is called Clip yr Orsedd, 'The Slope of the Throne': a judgement seat perhaps to oversee such games? Far-fetched it may seem to us but Sir John was convinced; could it be that he gave the name to the ridge? Would it be safer to assume that it is so named from more distant times and for quite different reasons?

The Greate Battayle to which Sir John refers would seem to be a reference to an early confrontation recorded between the Ordovices and a Roman cavalry unit, which was reported to have been annihilated.

The incident took place shortly before the arrival of Agricola as governor of Britain in 77 or 78 AD. Roman cavalry units were operating in North Wales between 74 and 77 AD, undertaking what would be described today as a policy of containment. As references to the incident describe the Roman unit as a cavalry regiment we must assume that it was an Ala. During the first years of the invasion these Alae were normally five hundred men but toward the end of the first century some were reinforced to produce units of a thousand. We have no means of telling whether this particular unit was of the larger or smaller version: my inclination would be toward the smaller.

The site of the battle is uncertain. The only clue to come from the historian Tacitus is that it took place 'in the territory of the Ordovices'. Exploratory work in the Meini Hirion / Braich-y-Dinas area has not produced any evidence to suggest that that, or any other battle ever took place in the vicinity.

Braich-y-Dinas and Pen-y-Dinas

Braich-y-Dinas is commonly translated as 'The Arm of the Fort' and also 'The arm of the City' and is applied to the promontory on which the village was built. Pen-y-Dinas, 'The summit of the fort or city' refers to the actual peak of the mountain. The use of Dinas as 'fort' in this particular case is perhaps not entirely accurate. The word Dinas is used here to refer to a fortified village. The old Britons called the Roman forts Caer. They also sometimes applied this name to their own forts but mainly used Dinas or a shortened version 'Din'; as in DinEiddin (Edinburgh). For the sake of clarity I intend to use Pen-y-Dinas, as this is the form of wording found in nearly all studies of the site. Fort, camp and fortified village will be used at random to refer to the same site as over the years different authorities have called it all of these.

In this chapter I hope to bring some life to the mountain which gave the village its name. A walk back through its history is a delightfully interesting journey. It offers something in the way of explanation but raises a thousand questions.

Early clues

In 1889 a new stone crushing mill was erected at Braich Llwyd, a site at the 500 ft contour and on the north eastern side of the mountain. In order to convey its output to the main railway line and jetty, a new tramway was built. It connected the work at

Braichllwyd with the main incline.

In March of 1890 a workman was set to work to trim and clean the sides of the tramway. On Friday the 21st of that month he found two urns. Unfortunately both were destroyed but whether that was the result of the clearing action or the ravages of centuries of exposure is not clear.

The find was reported to Mr Charles Darbishire. Mr Darbishire, as well as being the quarry owner, was a keen amateur antiquarian and his interest was immediately aroused by the urns. He ordered the work in that area to be halted until he had had an opportunity to gather together a small group of similarly interested gentlemen.

On March 27th work continued under the watchful eyes of Mr Darbishire's invited party. It did not take them long to discover that the route chosen for the new tramway had cut right through the end of a barrow. Although the mound measured some thirty feet by fifteen feet, its original height, though never very much, had been worn down to less than three feet above ground level.

Trenching in the mound revealed further vessels. Six further urns were found and five burials. Most of the urns were found turned upside down with their mouths resting on flat stones with a further stone above to act as a kind of rough protection from the pressure of the covering earth. The urns contained black earth and calcined bones and the soil around each one was also black, as if the urns had been used to contain the ashes on the very site where the cremations had taken place. The burning was so complete that no teeth or sliver of bone more than three or four inches was found. Those burials not contained in urns were scrutinised very carefully and it was decided that the complete lack of any sign of earthen ware or vessel of any kind indicated that they had never been contained and that the position in which they were found was exactly where and how they had been interred. All the urns were in a very fragile condition and handling was extremely difficult.

During the day a number of stones varying in size between eighteen inches and two and a half feet were found; they had been placed on the ground unevenly spaced and in an irregular circle. No urns but two or three burials were found within this enclosure.

The next dig took place on Tuesday, April the first. The excited group of antiquaries arrived at the scene to be met by nervous faces and the news that since the previous Thursday some men had visited the site and undertaken a private search. They had found an urn and smashed it in their search for, of all things, treasure! A true April fool's joke.

Somewhat chastened but undeterred, the official diggers continued. The final result was that one or two more unconfined burials were found and one other which differed from anything found up until then. This burial was of a different character altogether; the bones were in a shallow depression covered over by a thin slab of shale. That afternoon one further urn was discovered: it was inverted and in very good condition. It was about nine inches high and six inches across the mouth. The largest urn found during the excavations was about a foot high and nine inches across the mouth. A final and meticulous search was made in the hope of finding one or two small votive offerings or something similar. Even as the soil was returned to the barrow it was sifted and searched but it produced nothing.

On the following day work continued on the site but, as nothing more came to light it was agreed that all that could be done had been done and the workman carried on with his job of clearing and trimming the verges. According to Mr Charles H. Darbishire twenty one interments had been discovered. All, so far as could be made out, had been in urns of some description.

As the urns were in a precarious condition, somewhere had to be found where the temperature was fairly stable so that they and their contents, which were as yet undisturbed, could dry

View of Penmaenmawr with summit intact 1870

Penmaenmawr Promenade, 1918
(A.S. Evans)

Families on the Beach, Penmaenmawr in the 19th century
(A.S. Evans)

Penmaenmawr sands c. 1910 'Discretion a Dignity'
(A.S. Evans)

Sailing ships and coal burners at Penmaen Jetty
(A.S. Evans)

Quarry activities did not deter visitors
(A.S. Evans)

'The Sidings'
(A.S. Evans)

Coasters at Graiglwyd Jetty loading macadam for Kent CC
(A.S. Evans)

Picture showing destruction of the
axe producing ridge

Portrait of Col. Derbishire
(Gwynedd Archive Services)

Two 19th century prints, somewhat romanticised, emphasising the dangers of negotiating Pen-y-clip, Penmaenmawr (National Library of Wales)

Cist grave – Druids' Circle
(Crown Copyright: RCAHMW)

Main circle – Druids' Circle
(Crown Copyright: RCAHMW)

Ring cairn showing remains of stone and earth bank
(A.S. Evans)

71

Druids' Circle showing ancient track on right (A.S. Evans)

Small circle near Druids' Circle. The five stones might suggest an Irish influence. (A.S. Evans)

Stone alignments and remains of small circle – Druids' Circle (A.S. Evans)

Incense cup found near Braich Lwyd (Copyright: Chester City Council. Thanks are due to Chester City Council for making this material readily available)

Bronze Age burial urn found near Braich Lwyd (Copyright: Chester City Council. Thanks are due to Chester City Council for making this material readily available)

Bronze Age burial urn found near Braich Lwyd (Copyright: Chester City Council. Thanks are due to Chester City Council for making this material readily available)

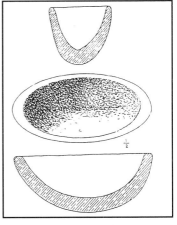

Scooped pebble cup found near Braich Lwyd (By kind permission of Archaeologica Cambrensis)

73

*This sketch, published in the 'Sphere' in 1909 shows the honeycomb effect
(Crown Copyright: RCAHMW)*

*Governor Pownall's sketch of 'The Cairn' on the summit of Pen-y-Dinas, as
sketched on the spot. Society of Antiquities 1769.
(Courtesy of the National Library of Wales)*

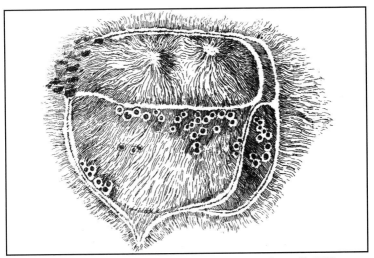

'A plan of the top of Penmaen Mawr', Governor Pownall, 1769 (Courtesy of the National Library of Wales)

Aerial view of Penmaenmawr in 1950 showing Hucks' probable route to the summit. From bottom right corner to point near modern viaduct and then straight up.

Work reaches the edge of the old village – traces of wall can be seen in top left. The scene that would have met Prof. Bosanquet in 1909
(By kind permission of National Museums and Galleries of Wales.
Department of Industry)

Mr W.D. Jones, Quarry manager, centre left in light jacket
(By kind permission of National Museums and Galleries of Wales.
Department of Industry)

This picture of drillers and work illustrates the futility of 'Keeping a look out' for small artifacts as suggested by the quarry owners and so summarily dismissed by Mr Harold Hughes. (By kind permisison of National Museums and Galleries of Wales. Department of Industry)

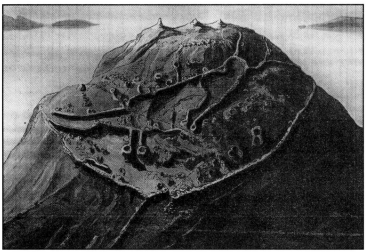

Artist's impression of Pen-y-Dinas for 'Sphere' magazine, 1909 (Gwynedd Archaeological Trust)

Picture of roofless hut from Richard Hughes' 1877 account
(Gwynedd Archaeological Trust)

Sketch of summit from Richard Hughes' 1877 account
(Gwynedd Archaeological Trust)

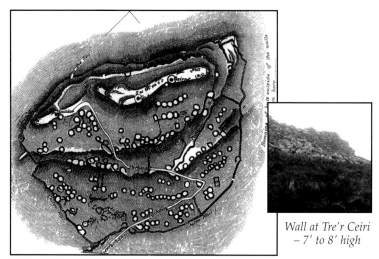

Wall at Tre'r Ceiri – 7' to 8' high

Plan of summit showing outline of defensive walls, pathways and huts. From Richard Hughes' 1877 account (Gwynedd Archaeological Trust)

Maen Amor
(A.S. Evans)

Looking east down the railway tracks.

View from Station Road East showing ships loading at two jetties.
Each jetty could accommodate two ships.

Gov. Pownall's impression of Penmaenmawr and Pen-y-Dinas from Llanfairfechan, 1769. (Courtesy of Gwynedd Archaeological Trust)

Showing expanse of circuit walls and demolished dwellings.

Hut circle showing entrance. Stick provides scale showing walls stil at about 5 to 6 feet in places.

Hut circles facing south/east

Pen-y-Dinas facing east

House circles showing one large house base and smaller attached.
Gentleman with cap is thought to be Harold Hughes.

House circles on Pen-y-Dinas facing east

Wall showing height of 6'-7'

Circuit wall showing thickness of approx 4-5 ft.

Hut circles facing south east. Pen-y-Perunaen farm is seen at the base of the summit.

Ancient hut bases on Penmaenmawr

Ancient hut/house base walls on Penmaenmawr

out. Where this took place is not clear.

After six weeks or so they had stabilised and all but one were transported to the Grosvenor Museum in Chester under the personal care of Mr Shrubsole, the Honorary Curator there. The journey was uneventful and all the vessels arrived safely. The one urn which did not go to Chester remained in Penmaenmawr on display in the coffee room of the Penmaenmawr Hotel, later to become The Grand Hotel. One can imagine that a cinerary urn complete with its contents, perched on a table is sure to have produced some animated comments among the village morning coffee set ! Which urn was left behind is not explained but I feel that in view of the fact that they had been claimed by a museum it would not have been one of the better examples.

When the urns were examined in Chester the contents were removed so that a search could be made for any funerary gifts which would normally have accompanied the dead. In two of the urns pins were found, one in each urn. They were made of bronze and were one and a half inches long.

In another a most unusual little vessel was found. It was made from a beach pebble which had been broken in half and the interior chiselled and scooped out. The vessel was four and a half inches long, two inches wide and stood one and a half inches high. This little cup aroused great interest as it was unlike any of the other finds. It was exhibited to the Society of Antiquaries in London where it caused great excitement and was declared to be absolutely unique. Mr Shrubsole entered into correspondence with The president of The Society of Antiquaries, Mr John Evans, Mr A.W. Franks FSA of the British museum and others but no one was aware of any such cup having been found anywhere else.

The smallest of the vessels found during the search of the barrows was described as an incense cup.

Also in the museum is a piece of Penmaenmawr stone one and a half inches thick and thirteen inches square which also caused some excitement, as to produce it would not only have required extraordinary skill but, in the opinion of the scholars and experts consulted, would also have needed a *metal* hammer!

It was intended that another barrow near to the first should also be explored but whether this ever took place I have not been able to find out. The articles described above are kept in the Grosvenor museum but are not on public display.

People

The burial mounds described in the previous chapter prompt us to ask, 'whose remains were in those urns?'

Are they the graves of villagers who had settled in the oak woods which then covered the slopes of the mountain? Other traces of occupation have been found in the fields at the foot of the mountain.

Alternatively, was there a fortification on the summit in the Bronze Age and were these the graves of some of its occupants? During the exploration of this mound another large mound was discovered nearby, perhaps indicating that the village, if there was one, was on or near that site for some years. Another explanation which could possibly be considered is that these two burial mounds contained dead from the summit settlement who had died of some kind of disease or illness and superstition had dictated that they be disposed of well away from the main site. When considering this latter possibility it must be borne in mind that it would have been a very difficult descent and there were more accessible areas nearby.

Nothing is known, or at least recorded, of the population of the village before Roman times. If there was a population, then a name for them is hard to find. The evidence of their existence or that of their ancestors or predecessors elsewhere on the moors has been discussed in the earlier chapters. It is on the ground and irrefutable. Any similarity between the two previous sites and the hilltop fort of Pen-y-Dinas ends there. The fort or fortified village we are about to discuss was obliterated many years ago. What is left of the mountain stands there now, an amputated stump, bleeding its history through massive man-made wounds.

We have no way of telling for certain whether the people who inhabited our fort were descendants of those who chipped the stone axes and erected the circle; or whether they were from a totally different source. The terms Celt and Celtic have been used in earlier accounts to describe the occupants of the village during the Roman occupation. I have continued this for convenience only because all the known tribes of the area during that time are invariably referred to in studies of the period as Celts. Further investigation of the site sometimes suggests that they might have been a more primitive indigenous race. As with the other two sites, when we delve further into the recorded evidence, we find that the questions we thought might be easily answered become obscured by contradictions, more questions are posed and fewer answers provided.

Fortunately, several characters from various periods in history have recorded their own impressions of the mountain and its history and these give us an idea of the magnitude of the defences before their erosion and destruction. They tell us little or nothing however of the occupants and their identity

We shall be looking at their impressions of this so called fortress and trying to build a picture of what might have been the story of Braich-y-Dinas. In particular we are indebted to those far seeing and determined gentlemen who, in the early years of the twentieth century, braved the elements to record the evidence while it existed. Without these valuable sources, factual and fanciful, there would be no canvas on which to paint our picture and no paint with which to colour it. Before dealing with Braich-y-Dinas in isolation it would be wise to look briefly at how the situation in Britain was developing.

Movement of peoples

Cross channel migration from the continent had been going on for thousands of years and each people brought with them new and usually improved methods of building, farming, animal husbandry and unfortunately, warfare. As each tribal wave or group of families was followed by the next the earlier settlers moved further inland and gradually the southern part of the island of Britain became quite heavily populated. The original inhabitants being either assimilated or dispossessed and forced further west and north.

The people who made these migratory journeys from the continental mainland were recognised under a number of names. The earliest probably walked across in small family groups while the land bridge was still intact, before the end of the last ice age some ten thousand years ago. Later came Celt-Iberians from Spain and the West Coast of France, followed for centuries after by a whole host of others. The word wave will be used to describe these movements and this invokes thoughts of hundreds or thousands storming ashore. This was not always so. Waves is a convenient word because it implies a steady happening, with regular intervals. Until the coming of Rome however these so called waves could have varied from small family groups to a tribal chief with his entourage and followers. A few traders perhaps or a hundred warriors. They came in a steady but irregularly sized flow and they formed tribes with names such as The Durotriges, The Atrebates, The Cantiaci, The Catuvellauni and so on. Some retained the name by which they were known before migration and which in some cases gave a clue to their place of origin. The Parisii are a good example of this. They settled in east Yorkshire but also gave their name to the present capital city of France.

It is of interest to note that these mass movements were going on for many years as the result of expanding populations resulting in the constant search for more and better land. Later, the movement of peoples was accelerated as the Roman Empire grew, not all however were hostile to Rome. Some, like the Brigantes in Yorkshire were openly allied.

At about 500 to 600 BC the flow increased; Gallic tribes, some under pressure from Rome, began to move across the channel from France and settled in what is now Southeast England. They brought with them further improvements in living standards as a result of contact with the newly emerging Roman State and other continental tribes. Technology had moved on. Stone and copper gave way to bronze and eventually to iron. The new materials produced ever finer domestic implements and a higher standard of living. These advances filtered slowly through the country as a result of development of trade and by tribal movement. Regretfully, together with these improvements emerged Man's need to dominate. In order to combat this, family groups banded together and became tribes. Small tribes then merged to become bigger tribes and so forth.

In what was to become Wales, the main tribes were the Silures, the Ordovices and the Demetae. On the Welsh marches, from mid Wales to the south lay the lands of the Dobbuni. From mid Wales to Chester the Cornovii held their territories. In the Northeast the Deceangli held what is now Clwyd and the old counties of Denbigh and Flint almost as far west as the Conwy river. At the Conwy the Decanti, a subsidiary of the Decanti people of Northern Scotland, had their centre. In Welsh history it appears as Arx Decantorum, stronghold of the Decantae. It is today's Deganwy. The smaller tribes of the Decangi and Cangani were recorded as holding the Llŷn peninsula in the west. Who was in Braich-y-Dinas? As the mountain lay more or less at the point where the lands of the northern tribes merged, it could have been any one or all three or four in turn.

The Ordovices were later, Brythonic Celts and were undoubtedly the numerically dominant tribe from mid-Wales northward, so it might have been they who held control of the mountain top even if they did not inhabit it but leased it so to speak to a lesser group under their control and protection. One or more of those lesser groups could have been indigenous folk whose ancestors made the journey to these islands when the land bridge existed thousands of years earlier. Professor Sheppard Frere has it that the Ordovices were possibly a confederacy of tribes rather than a single people and that Anglesey certainly was within their influence.

In order to avoid confusion, it would be convenient to clarify at this stage the differences between some of the different Celtic branches which eventually settled in Britain. On or about the beginning of the first millennium BC a common language had developed on the continent of Europe. Like all other languages it had regional differences. Over time however these differences were to become so pronounced that the Celts who had lived more or less as one people on the continent were later to invade Britain in two or more stages and as two distinct entities. The earlier waves of immigrants brought with them to Britain the language as it stood at the beginning of the first millennium BC. The next wave, some three or four hundred years later, brought with them a language which was heavily influenced by the Latin of the traders and soldiers of the expanding roman empire. By the time of the arrival in Britain of the second wave, the linguistic differences between the peoples of the two migrations might be compared with the Elizabethans of the 16th and 17th century being overtaken by the Victorians or even the people of the early 20th century.

Today the two branches are Known as P Celtic and Q Celtic. P Celtic is that spoken in Wales, Cornwall and Brittany. Q Celtic that which has survived in Ireland, the Scottish highlands and the Isle of man. In Scotland today traces of P Celtic are to be found in place names so it is likely that the two strains were used side by side in that area. An example of this is found in words such as *Gallt* (Slope), usually shortened today to *Allt* when used in everyday Welsh. Exactly the same word is used in the highlands to indicate a steep gradient. *More* in Scotland coincides with Mawr (Great) in Wales.

The reason for the attribution P and Q to the two branches is fairly straight forward. An easy illustration is the way in which the word for son or son of has developed. In Welsh and the other sections of P Celtic the word for son or son of, Mab has stayed as Mab or in older Welsh, Map, often reduced to Ap as in ap Dafydd, ap Llywelyn etc. In the Q section it has become Mac, the C being pronounced hard as in Q hence the name. There are other easily recognised instances. Pen for example, the Welsh word for Head or Chief retains the P whereas in Gaelic it becomes Cenn or Ceann with the C always sounded hard. There are many others which with a little thought become fairly obvious.

Which of these languages was spoken in the mountain refuge above Penmaenmawr all those years ago is anybody's guess but it's almost certain that a Welsh speaker today would recognise some of the words once the ear had become accustomed to what may have been a totally different accent and syllabic emphasis. Some of those words could have been the following:

Old Welsh/Celtic	Modern Welsh	English
Epo	Ebol	Colt
Cambo	Cam	Crooked
Abona	Afon	River
Verno	Gwern	Alder Grove/Marsh

Ordovices

The name Ordovices has been translated as, 'Hammer Fighters'.

Could the name indicate that they were perhaps not so advanced and still used stone hammers to fight? For the name to be so significant as to have given them an identity would suggest that they alone among the tribes used stone weapons. Having said that, we must not conclude that they did not also have weapons of bronze or iron. The name survives today in such place names as Dinorwic 'The town of the Ordovices' and the personal name 'Orwig'. Although the Ordovices might not have been at the forefront of technological advancement, under their control were people even less advanced. Were these the inhabitants of our village?

As unrest spread, compounds were built for the defence of family and property. Initially these were small enough to be defended by a family or family group; later these small defensive positions proved to be inadequate. In the fertile plains of the south, strategic hills were reinforced with massive earthen walls and deep ditches and were capable of containing thousands of people in time of danger. In the more remote uplands of the west and far north, the obvious choice was to choose the long, high hills on which to build their defences. They used the materials at hand to erect walls around the summit, sometimes earthworks surmounted by a wooden palisade, but more often a simple but sturdy dry stone wall.

To begin with these were nothing more than rough compounds built in a circle with an opening which could be blocked with thorns or a sturdy but primitive gate. In time however, they developed into huge complexes of several ramparts built in succession toward the summit. These were known as multivallate defences and covered several acres. The fortifications on Braich-y-Dinas were multivallate and measured about 950 ft from north to South and 700 ft from East to West. They covered an area of a little over ten acres. The dwellings were often scooped levels on which huts and small yards were enclosed and terraced into the natural slope of the hill. Some of the huts were single, others were grouped into small cells not unlike a small honeycomb. It was this form of fortified village that crowned Braich-y-Dinas.

Before we look in detail at the defences on the summit of Penmaenmawr's mountain, let us consider what others before us have made of them.

Famous visitors

Perhaps the earliest mention that could possibly be regarded as relating to the fortifications was made by Hywel ap Owain Gwynedd in the twelfth century AD. In a poem dated 1170 he refers to 'The proud towers of 'Gyfylchi'. I have not been able to confirm that the bard was alluding to the ruins on Pen-y-Dinas when he wrote those words or whether he was referring to a mystical and perhaps mythical palace supposed to have existed at the foot of Alltwen where his wife was apparently hiding from the Anglo Norman invaders. His name is carried today in the place name Myrddin Hywel below St Gwynin's church.

In Camden's Britannia there is an account of the fortifications, taken from the manuscripts of Sir John Wynne of Gwydir in the time of Charles the first 1625-1649.

In his description Sir John tells us that he saw, 'Ruinous walls of an exceeding strong fortification, compassed with a treble wall, and within each wall, the foundations of at least one hundred towers, about six yards in diameter within the walls. This castle was (while it stood) impregnable: there being no way to offer any assault on it, the hill being so very high, steep and rocky, and the walls of such strength. The way or entrance into it ascending with many turnings, so that one hundred men might defend themselves against a whole legion: and yet it would seem that there were lodgings within those walls for twenty thousand men.'

The antiquarian Edward Lluyd left us this report from 1698. 'A lofty impregnable hill on the top of Penmaenmawr, the fort encompassed by a treble wall and within each wall the foundation of at least one hundred towers, all around and about six yards in diameter. It seems there were lodgings here for twenty thousand. Within the innermost there is a well giving water in the driest summer. The strongest fort in all Snowdon. There a hundred men may defend themselves against a legion.' This need not necessarily be considered an eyewitness account, bearing as it does such a close, almost word for word, resemblance to that of Sir John Wynne.

1771 saw yet another ascent of Penmaenmawr and by yet another gentleman-antiquarian. This time it was Governor Pownall, sometimes presented as Pownell, 1722-1805.

A noted colonial administrator and one time governor of Massachusetts, he was originally from Lincoln. Pownall spent his later years back in Britain and became known as something of an able if inflexible antiquarian. In the third volume of the Archaeologia, Pownall describes his first and presumably only, ascent of Penmaenmawr. It can be deduced from his account that like many other travellers of the time he based himself at Ty'n y Penmaen inn at Gerizim. I would suggest that the following brief extract betrays the fact that the governor already held pre conceived and rather uncomplimentary ideas about Pen-y-Dinas.

'As I stopped to bait my horses at the small inn at the foot of Penmaenmawr, I took that opportunity of going to the top of the mountain in search of this singular and curious fortress as it is called and described.' The tone of his writing and his choice of words imply that he was only going to have a look because he was passing and thought he would amuse himself by seeing just enough of the walls to confirm his already formed opinion.

His climb was made more disagreeable by the fact that he was, as he says, 'Winded' by the gradient and the pace that his guide was setting. His guide was the poor hermit who maintained the road around the headland, depending on the generosity of the travellers for his living: as such he was no doubt at ease with the climb.

From Pownall's description it would appear that he was taken up the Llanfairfechan side of the mountain. His troubles were exacerbated when, having achieved the summit he found it wreathed in damp cloud and mist.

By now thoroughly uncomfortable, he sketched the summit and the walls and confidently declared, 'It was never a fortification!' He was of the opinion that the innermost enclosure was some kind of druidic sepulchre. The Cambrian Traveller's Guide of 1813 insists that the governor said that this view was supported by the presence of what he described as a 'Long Barrow' within the enclosure and attached to the sepulchre: that there was not enough room for habitation and that the walls could never have been used to fight from. This would fit with my earlier question regarding a possible hierarchy of priests or the like and their likely living quarters. The governor did say however that he would 'await Mr Pennant's survey,' referring to an impending visit by Thomas Pennant and that he expected much from that 'great antiquary's survey.'

It has to be said that the walls would probably *not* have withstood a sustained attack by organised and well-equipped forces such as the Roman army. On the other hand the British or Celtic way of attack was not to slowly but surely winkle out defenders or shower them with stones and sharp missiles from siege artillery. Records show that almost without exception a British charge was formidable and if it worked, carried all before it, if unsuccessful it was followed by a withdrawal and only rarely repeated. If the walls were not surmounted or penetrated the first time then further efforts could well have been half hearted. Sling stones rocks and spears, all hurled from higher ground and from behind walls could well have discouraged a second attempt.

On the seaward side the severe slopes of Braich-y-Dinas leading up to the walls of the village were thickly strewn with sharp edged boulders and scree. This natural defence served as a ready made chevaux de frise and would have rendered walking difficult and a full-blooded charge impossible. On the landward side however, the approach from the Southeast was up a relatively gentle slope and across clear open ground. Two defensive walls countered this apparent weakness. Quarrying activity had removed all traces of a possible third wall before a survey in 1909 could be carried out. From the West, the citadel ridge, even if only surmounted by a low wall, would still have provided a formidable obstacle.

A report published by The Royal Commission on the Ancient and Historical Monuments of Wales c. 1970 gave the walls to be 8 to 15 feet thick and with a maximum height of 9 feet. (This was considered to be their approximate thickness and height when first built). They were without wall walks. This might appear as a disadvantage until one recalls that as the encampment was built in terraces, the defenders would have been able to see over the walls whereas any attacker probably would not. Irregular paths crossed the interior with partially concealed entrances at different stages. The defences were undoubtedly there to keep *somebody* out rather than, or perhaps as well as, animals in.

In 1773 and 1776, Thomas Pennant made three tours through Wales. The following are extracts from his description of his visits to Braich-y-Dinas during those years.

'I have more than once visited the summit of this noted rock, to view the fortifications described by the editor of *Camden*, from some notes of that sensible old baronet Sir John Wynne of Gwedir, and have found his account very just . . . After climbing for some space among the loose stones, the fronts of three if not four walls presented themselves very distinctly one above the other. In most places the facings appeared very perfect, but all of dry work. I measured the height of one wall, which was at the time nine feet; the thickness seven feet and a half.' Interestingly Pownall had also measured the walls and whereas Pennant gave nine feet, the governor says they were only five feet high.

Pennant goes on, 'Between these walls in all parts were innumerable small buildings, mostly circular, and regularly faced within and without, but not disposed in any certain order, these had been much higher as is evident from the fall of stone, which lie scattered at their bottoms; and probably had the form of towers as Sir *John* asserts. Their diameter in general is from twelve to eighteen feet; but some were far less, not exceeding five feet. The walls were in places intersected with others equally strong. On the north-west and south-east are the plain marks of two roads of a zig-zag form, with the remains of walls on both sides which lead to the summit. On the small area of the top had been a small group of towers, or cells like the former; one in the centre and five others surrounding it. Three are still distinct; of the two others are only faint vestiges. Near this had been I believe, a similar group, but at present reduced to a shapeless heap of stones. Near one of these groups is a well cut in the live rock, and always filled with water, supplied by the rains and kept full by the frequent impending vapours . . . This (site) was most judiciously chosen to cover the passage into Anglesey and the remoter part of their country; and must, from its vast strength, have been invincible, except by famine, being inaccessible by its natural steepness toward the sea and on the other parts fortified in the manner described.'

A shaky story

In the summer of 1794, Joseph Hucks, a young gentleman from Yorkshire undertook a walking tour of Wales. His companion on the expedition was Samuel Taylor Coleridge, later to become famous in the world of poetry and romanticism. The party later became four when Hucks and his companion were joined at Conwy by two other travellers with similar intentions, Mr

Brooke and Mr Berdmore. Their route took them along the North Wales coast to Abergwyngregyn where they stayed at the inn. It is likely that the inn in question is that one now between the A55 and the sea shore.

The following day they undertook to climb Penmaenmawr and the following passages from their accounts of the ascent are those which I have considered valuable to this study of Braich-y-Dinas.

It should be pointed out that in those days, having reached the foot of the mountain they would have started their climb, not from the level of today's road but probably from the Ty'n y Penmaen on the old road much lower down at Gerizim. This start point would have put them directly under the steep crags visible from the present road, but would also have allowed them to see the alternative, gentler route to their right, around the mountain to the west. From where they stood, the track, such as it was, climbed steeply up to the left, that is toward Penmaenmawr village and continued eastward in a series of zigzags until it reached a pathway higher up which then led to the East toward Conwy. It must be assumed that youth and the spirit of adventure persuaded them to tackle the more dangerous route, along the track for a way and then, having reached the path to Penmaenmawr, directly up the face!

Mr Hucks takes up the narrative 'We rose early the following morning . . . We rashly took the resolution to venture up this stupendous mountain without a guide and therefore unknowingly fixed upon the most difficult part to ascend. At length we surmounted every danger and difficulty, and arrived safely at the top; but the fatigue we had undergone, and the excessive heat of the day, deprived us, in a great degree of that pleasure we should otherwise have received from the prospect, and occasioned a tormenting thirst that we were not able to gratify; for water was an article we searched for in vain.' It has been frequently suggested that the inspiration for the famous lines in the 'Rime of the Ancient Mariner' 'Water, water everywhere, nor any drop to drink.' Came from Coleridge's experiences on Penmaenmawr when, though faced by the great expanse of seawater he could find none to drink!

Having achieved their aim of reaching the summit they decided to return. 'Preparing in the utmost despondency to descend, we accidentally turned over a large flat stone that concealed a little spring, which, thus obstructed, became absorbed under the surface of the earth. The parched-up soldiers of Alexander's army could not have felt greater joy in the discovery of his little treasure than we did of ours. In the course of our descent we incautiously separated: and as it was dusk, I began to be under some apprehension that we might lose ourselves in the intricacies of the mountain; in order to discover their direction from me, I frequently repeated their names and was much entertained with a beautiful echo which returned the sound of my voice in three different directions.'

In a letter to a Henry Martin on the twenty second of July 1794, Coleridge does not mention Hucks in his description of the climb, thereby casting some doubt upon the authenticity of Hucks' account.

Hucks' own description of the descent with its mention of echoes and hooting owls and screeching buzzards simply does not hold together either. One is a nocturnal bird the other a daytime high flier. It would be unlikely that he would hear them both together unless of course one or the other were roosting and he disturbed them in a clumsy descent. Over the years, in letters to friends Coleridge often repeated the incident of the finding of the spring but, like Huck in his correspondence never mentions the fortifications. How strange!

Contrary to the facts

In 1804 the Reverend W. Bingley published a description of his excursions through North Wales during the summers of 1798 and 1801. The Reverend was a fellow of the Linnean Society and describes himself as being 'Late of Peterhouse, Cambridge'. As all other travellers did in those days, he went to see the enclosures on Braich-y-Dinas. He deduced that the circular remains were of 'soldiers' ' huts and the cairns on the summit he thought were once watchtowers. He describes the well on the summit as being small and square: and despite the very hot dry weather, held 'a considerable quantity of water'. This is a rare allusion to the shape of the well but once again there are no measurements, he simply calls it small. He is quite clear in his description: he says well and makes no reference to a spring.

It was the reverend gentleman's opinion that Governor Pownall was 'contrary to the facts' and 'contrary to commonly received opinion' when he said that Braich-y-Dinas was never intended to be defended. One wonders whether even that worthy man of the cloth was inclined to be swept along with the popular viewpoint because it fitted into the image of the 'Noble Savage' then prevalent, whereas the governor would have been inclined to see from a soldier's viewpoint the impracticality of defending such a site in the event of a prolonged siege. Perhaps there was an element of truth in both versions.

The following account is based on a series of manuscripts, now in the Cardiff City library which were published in 1917 as *Tours in Wales 1804 – 1813 by Richard Fenton:*

Richard Fenton and a party of friends were conducting a tour of Wales in 1810 and by Friday the 20th. of July had reached Caerhun where they explored the church and the remains of Kanovium the Roman fort there. Saturday saw them making their way over the Sychnant pass where they took time to inspect Castell Caer Lleion on Mynydd Maes-y-Dre (Conwy mountain).Eventually they came to the road around the headland of Penmaenmawr where all were suitably overawed by the rocky crags above and the crashing waves below.

Sunday was spent at Aber.

Monday July 23rd. dawned fair and Mr Fenton and friends set out on an excursion to the top of Penmaenmawr. 'We had looked forward' he says, 'with much curious expectation from the accounts of it by Edward Lhuyd, and after him, by all historians and tourists ever since, though I doubt much if half of those who mention it have ever seen it. The description of it by Edward Lhuyd is certainly exaggerated.'

Fenton continued his commentary as he reached the summit crest. Here he said he saw two 'Large Carneddau' in one of which that had been opened he declares he saw the remains of a Cistvaen. Carneddau are cairns; not the small heap which is often found on hilltops but a man-made covering for a burial. They can be thirty or so feet long and half as wide. This does not somehow fit the other descriptions and pictures of the cairns on Pen-y-Dinas. There are two large cairns on Braich-y-Dinas, but some considerable distance from where the summit would have been.

The Welsh word carnedd is what gives this particular range of hills its name 'Y Carneddau'; a study of the mountain names will reveal Carnedd Dafydd, Carnedd Llywelyn etc. Cist (Pron. Keest) is chest in Welsh and Vaen is an Anglicised version of Faen, a derivative of Maen, 'stone'; hence stone chest.

The Cistvaen he mentioned is a slabsided burial chest. No other account mentions this Cistvaen and it is not until Harold Hughes' excavation after the First World War that any reference is made to any trace of possible burial on the summit and even after scientific examination it is simply described as dust, with no mention of a Cistvaen.

The well is mentioned briefly and Fenton is inclined to accept Pennant's mist and rain explanation for the constant water.

One extremely interesting thing is mentioned as they make their way down from the summit. Fenton says 'We observe at the base of the high mountain a circular building, which on examining, I found had no aperture or opening on the sides, and though now uncovered, appeared *(at one time)* to have ended in a cove, like the top of an oven, and was perfect beyond the part that had begun to contract into an arch.' In this case 'the base of the high mountain' refers to that area which is at the bottom of the summit peak and not to the bottom of the mountain proper. It was his opinion too that circles on the Conwy side of the apex of the mountain were originally constructed in a similar way. He offered no explanation for their use. I will draw the reader's attention to this method of hut building at a later stage.

Some 40 years later in 1843, Edward George Lytton Bullwer, 1st Baron Lytton, popularly known as Edward, Lord Lytton, published a novel called Harold, The last of the Saxon Kings, in which the defences atop Penmaenmawr are described. The following are extracts from that account, which is supposedly based on fact but is liberally laced with measures of imagination.

'Nor is it marvellous that at that day there should be disputes as to the nature and strength of that supposed bulwark, since, in times the most recent, and among antiquaries the most learned, the greatest discrepancies exist, not only as to the theoretical opinion but plain matter of observation, and simple measurement.' The description goes on . . . 'The place I need say was not as we see it now, with its foundations of gigantic ruin affording ample space for conjecture: yet, even then, a wreck as of Titans, its date and purpose was lost in remote antiquity.' It is interesting to see that even among the enlightened there was no idea whatsoever as to the identity of the builders of the fort or of its purpose.

'The central area . . . formed an oval barrow of loose stones: whether so left from the origin, or the relics of some vanquished building was unknown even to bard and diviner. Round this space were four strong circular vallations of loose stones with a space about eighty yards between each; the walls themselves generally about eight feet wide, but of various height, as the stones had fallen 'by time and blast'. Along these walls rose numerous and almost countless buildings which might pass for towers, though only a few had been recently and rudely roofed in. To the whole of this quadruple enclosure there was but one narrow entrance, now left open as if in scorn of assault; and a narrow winding pass down the mountain, with innumerable curves, alone led to the single threshold. Far down the hill, walls again were visible; and the whole surface of the steep soil, more than halfway in the descent was heaped with vast loose stones, as if the bones of some dead city. But beyond the innermost enclosure of the fort rose thick and frequent, other mementos (sic) of the Briton; many cromlechs already shattered and shapeless; the ruins of stone houses and high overall those upraised mighty amber piles as at Stonehenge . . . All, in short showed that the name of this place "The Head of the City", told its tale; all announced that, there, once the Celt had his home and the gods of the druid their worship . . . and in the vessel, full and clear, the water from the spring that bubbled up everlastingly through the bones of the dead city. Beyond this innermost space, round a basin of rock, through which the stream overflowed as from an artificial conduit lay the wounded.'

It should be allowed that this description is likely to have been greatly influenced by what he had read of the summit and by what his imagination told him the place might have been like on or about the eleventh century.

Consider the following. The Transactions of the Society of Cymmrodorion of London, a much-respected body, published in 1882 what it referred to as 'The present theory that Dinas Penmaen was originally a druidical place of Worship before becoming a British fortress.'

The numerous remains of circles, cairns and burial mounds near the base of its summit, its close proximity to Anglesey and its position overlooking the island would have made this theory acceptable. When the writer goes on to describe Dinas Penmaen however, the result is confusion, rendering its usefulness as a verbal guide at best dubious.

Despite the good intentions of the society or perhaps its representative, this account leans heavily on legend and local folk tales and is subsequently suspect as a historical version of events. It also displays a lack of personal knowledge of the area, which suggests that the piece was heavily dependent upon earlier accounts, resulting in mistakes, which someone familiar with the area would not make. Some of the translations of Welsh place names are also hopelessly inaccurate.

In its opening paragraphs for instance, it tells us that, 'The few positive facts about Dinas Penmaen are these: It is 'A hill 1553 ft high.' It then goes on to say that 'Braich-y-Ddinas terminates in a British fortress in which is a well of spring water. This Dinas is one mile from Dinas Penmaen.' The writer is obviously awry here and is referring to the same mountain or hill but appears to believe that Pen-y-Dinas and Dinas Penmaen are separate and that she is writing about a different location. The alternative location, which caused the confusion, is possibly Castell Caer Lleion above Conwy, or Dinas, above Llanfairfechan, which has a similar name but is nowhere near so high.

In view of this rather serious error it would be unwise, however tempting, to give too much credence to the description of the well with its measurements of 'three or four feet deep for rainwater.' It is unfortunate, as they are the only measurements offered by anyone in their accounts and descriptions. There is no mention of a spring, but again the claim that the well was dependent on rainwater. That of course would coincide with Pennant's version, but does not square with her earlier claim that 'Braich-y-Ddinas terminates in a British fort in which is a well of spring water'.

The piece continues and mentions many names which imply

suffering, Bryn Du, 'Black Mound' is one: Bryn Dyoddef (sic) correctly *Dioddef*, meaning 'The Hill Or Mound of Suffering' is another. The author would have us believe that the sources of this information are mountain shepherds who say that the mounds are so called because 'People were killed to please false gods,' or, 'people of the bad religion used to kill and burn people here.' This last is interesting. Although the 'shepherds' are supposed to have told the author of these happenings, where did they obtain their information? It could either have been passed down over the years, growing as it did so or, assuming the 'shepherds' could read, they in turn could have seen the incidents referred to elsewhere. If the latter is the case then the 'shepherds' were simply telling the author what other writers had already told them. The fascinating part about all this is, if the stories were folklore how did they know of the burning? Is it possible that the happenings at Druids' Circle could have survived over three thousand years of retelling and still have retained such a degree of accuracy? Was it pure coincidence? Cremation was confirmed at Druids' Circle only after excavation in 1958. Had farmers or herdsmen accidentally or deliberately disturbed the mounds and come to their own conclusion and as a result devised their own theories about bad gods?

The Cambrian Traveller's Guide of 1813 has an interesting snippet among otherwise repeated information from the sources already covered. It claims that Governor Pownall said that 'In the enclosure is a barrow of the kind which Dr Stukely calls a Long Barrow and attaches to the sepulchre of an arch druid.' It is difficult to reconcile this with the fact that nobody else ever mentioned a barrow *within* the walls.

These, observations, interesting as they may be, have about them the feel of the age of the romantics, with the exception perhaps of Pennant who was an accomplished historian and more meticulous in his appraisal.

The 'Romantic' movement of the nineteenth century, with its

devotion to the use of imagination, intuition and emotion was hardly suited to the description and appraisal of historical evidence. Among its greatest advocates were Samuel Taylor Coleridge and Lord Byron, whose accounts have been discussed here. The movement was responsible for a revival of Celticism. All things Celtic were revered. Celtic dress was re invented, including that of the modern bards of the Eisteddfod, without too much emphasis on accuracy. Ancient sites were visited and books written, again without regard for fact when fancy was more attractive. To the disciples of Romanticism, Braich-y-Dinas and the surrounding hills with their wealth of standing stones, circles, tumuli and huts, were irresistible

Romanticism had little foothold outside the circles of the moneyed elite however: it did not feed hungry families, neither could it protect the old mountain. The engineers and hardheaded moneymakers had now entered the story and were about to engage the ancient fortification in a battle it could neither win, nor survive!

The road to extinction

The opening moves

In the first report of The Royal commission of Ancient Monuments in Wales and Monmouthshire published in 1910, it was revealed that the enquiries made to His Majesty's Office of Woods and Forests discovered that Penmaenmawr Mountain had been leased to that department for 52 years commencing on the 10th of October 1899 for the purpose of quarrying stone. Prior to the 1910 report however, fears had already been voiced about the preservation of the walls and huts. Surely, such an important historical site would be protected?

In order to gain a clearer picture of the situation on the mountain, Professor R.C. Bosanquet, on behalf of the Commission, had been asked to visit the mountain and submit a report. Professor Bosanquet was a widely travelled and highly regarded historian and academic whose inclusion in the undertaking could be expected to produce opinions and arguments that would add weight to the proceedings.

On the 22nd of May 1909, and accompanied by the Secretary of the commission, the professor arrived in Penmaenmawr. The two men soon found that quarrying on the north slopes was already at the lower limits of the fortifications. It was their opinion that in the course of time, work would be extended so as to eventually clear away the whole of the summit.

As early as eighteen ninety-eight, a working floor level or bank was opened on Penmaenmawr at one thousand three hundred and twelve feet. Named Kimberley in commemoration of the South African town later besieged during the Boer War, it was, by nineteen hundred and nine, to bring the quarry right in among those huts and relics which were only just outside the perimeter walls of the main camp. To illustrate the rate at which rock was being removed from the mountain and give some idea of the sense of urgency and approaching catastrophe that must have haunted those representatives of the Royal Commission, consider this. Four years later, in nineteen thirteen, it was revealed that during those operations, forty five tons of gunpowder and seven and a half tons of high explosive had removed five hundred and seventeen thousand tons of rock in one year alone. Over half of that had been taken from the workings immediately below the fort. Time was certainly not on the side of the historians!

On the 17th June, shortly after the visit by Mr Bosanquet, during questions in the House of Commons, Mr Llewelyn Williams, MP for the district, asked Mr Hobhouse, Financial Secretary for the Treasury whether the Commissioners for Woods and Forests had 'leased the mountain, including the site of 'The Roman or Prehistoric camp' to a firm of quarry workers without reservation of the land occupied by the camp, or any conditions for its scientific exploration during its gradual destruction.' During the course of his reply, Mr Hobhouse said, 'It is a fact that the site of these remains is not reserved . . . *but the lessees do not intend to disturb the actual camp*' . . . (Author's italics and emphasis) Mr Hobhouse went on 'but as the undertaking gives employment to 600 men I do not think Commissioners of Woods would be warranted in interfering on this point, even if they had the power to do so!'

It appeared then that the government was really rather indifferent to the activities to save some rather remote Welsh hill fort. They were to be surprised by the tenacity and determination of the historical organisations to fight their corner.

As there appeared to be a discrepancy between the statement made in the house by the Financial secretary and the report submitted by Professor Bosanquet, the commissioners thought a second visit by the Professor to the site might be advisable.

The subsequent visit was made on 9th August, 1909. During this visit Professor Bosanquet interviewed the manager of the Penmaen quarry, Mr W.D. Jones. Mr Jones said that so far as he was aware, *there was no intention of altering any of the arrangements for the working of the quarry with the view of saving any portion of the ancient fortification.* Dismayed by this answer and on making further investigation, the professor found that the destruction of the lowest of the camp walls on the north side had begun since his last visit and was proceeding before his eyes. It was explained to him that the development of the quarry could not in fact be carried on without the gradual sacrifice of the camp.

At that point, and for some reason, which will be forever unknown, the quarry proprietors, The Brundrit Coy. appeared to modify their position and explained to Professor Bosanquet that although it would be impossible to continue quarrying without destroying the remains, as long as the survey work and excavation was undertaken by a responsible body, they would be happy to give any assistance that might be required. This offer was to include every facility and they even instructed their workmen to report any finds.

On the face of it this offer seems quite reasonable but the quarry workers, who, though they undoubtedly respected and appreciated the benefits of education, were not themselves educated men; they were there to work to support families. How could they have been expected to know what was of importance? Even had they known, would they have lost valuable time reporting any find, assuming they were able to recognise one? Time was money to them and very little at that. Every penny counted. Besides, there was no mention of any reward for such services.

Professor Bosanquet remained despondent. He reported despondently, 'As matters are, there is no hope of saving one of the finest prehistoric fortifications in the British Isles from ultimate annihilation'. The situation looked grim.

That same evening, a meeting of The Cambrian Archaeological Association, of which the Professor was a member, was held at Chester. At this meeting, a resolution was adopted that Mr Harold Hughes ARIPA, of Bangor should be requested to undertake on behalf of the association, a survey of the camp. Mr Hughes was a member of the Cambrian Archaeology Society. In 1903 he had been engaged on a survey and excavation of Tre'r Ceiri on Yr Eifl, a site very similar in date and construction to Pen-y-Dinas. Threatened by quarrying, though not to the same degree as Penmaenmawr's hillfort, it was an important site and warranted recording.

When contacted and asked by the secretary of the Cambrian Association whether he would be willing to help, Mr Hughes replied that he was already engaged on just such a survey in Penmaenmawr. Dismissive of the Quarry owners' palliative regarding finds, he said, 'I believe there was an idea of someone in the quarry keeping a lookout in case anything turned up, The result, I believe, would be nil'. Mr Hughes' early start on the mountaintop must rank among the foremost of individual initiatives and was eventually to put on record for Wales, an important site whose history would otherwise have been irretrievably lost.

The survey of the site, this time with official backing, continued in 1909. This was followed over a number of years by a series of detailed excavations, the details of which are explored in a later chapter.

Some idea of how important Braich-y-Dinas was considered to be in archaeological and historical circles and in the world of academia can be gleaned from the fact that an account of the happenings in Penmaenmawr appeared in The **Sphere** of 1909.

The Sphere was a magazine that might be compared to The National Geographic Magazine of today. Shortly after the nature of activity on the mountain became known, the magazine sent a reporter and an artist to gather the facts. The artist's impression of the peak with its fortifications can be seen on the rear cover. The sketch of a roofless hut also appeared, this was copied directly from a drawing that appeared in Mr Richard Hughes' survey of 1877.

This early survey was proposed by Mr Richard Hughes but carried out by Mr W.G. Haslam. The drawings were made by Mr W.G. Smith.

Even as the archaeologists struggled with the elements on the bleak summit, the correspondence went on and discussions were held between departments and in Parliament An entry from file W 4075 dated 4 January, 1912 from the offices in Whitehall of H.M. Woods and Forests, listing a number of sites in North Wales with mining or quarrying potential, is of interest as it shows that with regard to Braich-y-Dinas, the following was written. 'This is partly on Crown waste land and partly on land sold by the crown many years ago to Mr Darbishire reserving minerals. The area is included in the lease of the Penmaenmawr Quarries.The lease contains no provision for the preservation of the camp.' The last sentence was already known to the archaeological Society and its diggers, but now, interestingly, the letter also contained the following rider; apparently dated sometime later than the original list, 'Crown mineral leases now contain covenants on the part of the lessees not to injure or disturb or permit to be injured or disturbed any objects of archaeological or historical interest.' Almost as if to protect Sir Stafford Howard KCB, the head of department, the writer of the letter, a Mr Evans, had added, 'The Ordnance maps purport to shew many such items as to which he has no special information and of the authenticity or importance of which he is unable to judge.'

It was an unheralded but important victory for the

Cambrian Archaeological Society. Too late to save Braich-y-Dinas, it would ensure the preservation, or at least the recording before destruction, of other similar places of historical value. The preceding chapters are important because they reveal how valuable this site was considered to be. They also serve to show how easily sites of historical importance can be lost through apathy reinforced by the machinations of government and industry, often without the general public even realising that such places had ever existed.

The survey and excavation

Towards the end of 1909 permission was granted by the quarry proprietors for the initial survey to go ahead. Harold Hughes, armed with little more than the basics of nineteenth or early twentieth century surveying equipment, together with a notebook, sketchpad and some pencils, took his first official steps into the world of ancient Penmaenmawr. Mr Willoughby Gardner, a member of the Archaeologia Cambrensis committee and a competent and experienced historian and archaeologist in his own right, joined the survey team on two occasions and the Rev. J.C.Hughes, for the whole week. They did not have an easy time of it.

According to Mr Hughes' report, 'Practically every day devoted to the survey has been unfortunate in respect of the weather. At the best, a high and cold wind has been blowing; at the worst, operations have been rendered impossible, due to heavy rain.' Without the benefit of modern equipment or even today's warm shower proof clothing the little group of one professional and two or three enthusiasts began what must have seemed like a Herculean task. It was imperative however that all the remaining walls and entrances should be identified and recorded; at least then an accurate plan of the fort could be drawn.

Work started on this first project as soon as was possible and by April 1912, Mr Hughes could report in the Archaeologia Cambrensis that 'The summit, with a considerable length of the NW fortifications, and their return on the NE have, so far, been plotted.' (Fig. 6). The summit was crowned with two large cairns and one much smaller. One was dilapidated, a second was used by the Ordnance survey as a trigonometrical station and it was Mr Hughes' opinion that because of that they had restored it. It could therefore no longer be considered as part of the ancient structure. A well lay between and slightly west of the cairns. The third cairn was sadly dilapidated and only fragments remained. The central, that is the reconstructed cairn occupied the true summit of the mountain, which at that time was 1550 ft.

Interestingly, according to Pennant, 'A Mr Caswell, at the request of Mr Flamstead the great astronomer, measured the height, and found it to be 1545ft.' The Mr Flamstead was presumably Mr John Flamsteed, 1646-1719, the first Astronomer Royal of England.

Mr Hughes's report further indicates that there were three surrounding walls except in those places where they had appeared to be already quarried away. In view of this Mr Hughes applied the caution of science and on his survey plan has marked walls as being in existence only where they are physically recognisable as walls. When reading these survey drawings it should be noted that where there is *any* element of doubt, the outer faces are shown as dotted lines and the walls shown hatched in. Walls are only shown as a black line where an actual dressed face is identifiable. To the lay mind, the black lines might not amount to very much but when one considers the age of the walls and their convenience as a source of building and dry walling material: it is a miracle that any survived for so long! It was also Mr Hughes' opinion that there was no Roman influence to be found in the construction of the walls.

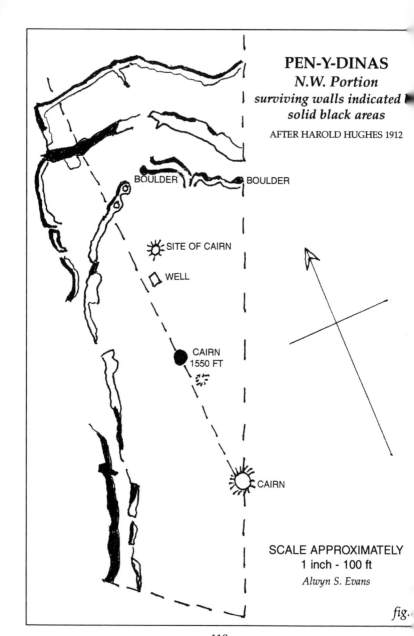

PEN-Y-DINAS
N.W. Portion
surviving walls indicated
solid black areas

AFTER HAROLD HUGHES 1912

BOULDER

BOULDER

SITE OF CAIRN

WELL

CAIRN
1550 FT

CAIRN

SCALE APPROXIMATELY
1 inch - 100 ft
Alwyn S. Evans

fig.

118

At this point it is considered convenient to insert an overview of the site as seen and sketched by W.G. Smith in 1877. The sketch is not meant to provide an absolutely accurate plan of the site, simply a general idea of how the site looked before its demolition. One important piece of information that the image does show is that the site was on a slope to the Southeast and not perched on the summit in a uniform manner as could easily be imagined and as is often implied. Building the village in such a way meant that it was given some protection from the prevailing winds for most of the year. In fact the walled part of the village occupied some three hundred feet of the slope downwards from the summit. Many other huts were to be found dotted around the mountain top outside the protected area but nearly all were on the sheltered, that is the west and south west side.

At an urgently convened meeting of the Committee of the Cambrian Archaeological Association at Abergele, It was agreed that as time was short a grant should be made so that the excavations could now take place as the survey continued. The proprietors of the quarry were approached and their permission asked to excavate within the walls. Messrs. Brundrit and Co., the owners, readily agreed. Mr J.H. Higson, the managing director and Colonel Johnson were outstanding in their kindness. They made arrangements for men, usually employed in the quarry, to work under Mr Hughes' direction. Their pay was presumably organised by Mr Hughes from grants paid to the Cambrian Archaeological Society. *This was a considerably enlightened attitude on the part of the quarry owners, which stood in stark contrast to the barely disguised irritation and lack of concern shown by the London based officialdom at the beginning of the affair.* The italics are the author's.

Work began in earnest on the site in September 1911 and continued for one week, from the 18th to the 23rd. During this time, five huts were explored and several items were unearthed. Meagre as these finds turned out to be, they were to

119

shed the first faint, flickering, glimmers of light on the story of Braich-y-Dinas. Although many finds were made in several huts over a number of years, it is not intended to describe each hut or each find in detail, or to give its position unless the significance of the find warrants it. Once the general descriptions of the huts, regarding width length and possible height are made at the beginning, these can be applied with very little variation to the remainder.

The first hut chosen was known as 'The double hut' because of its unusual building form. It was situated within and close to the second rampart and position is marked 'a' on the sketched plan. The hut had been built on a foundation of loose scree. The hard ground outside the entrance was 2ft 4 ins lower than the threshold while the rear of the building was built up to the sloping ground at its rear.

This method of creating platforms was found to have been used in nearly all the surviving huts. The lower wall in this case was reinforced with a shorter, wider wall that created a step effect. The doorway to the hut was a little less than 4ft wide and faced Southeast, as was the case in the majority of the other huts. This of course meant that they would avoid the worst of the howling winter winds and the driving rain. The entrance gave immediate access to the lower chamber and was connected to the upper by a short passage some four feet long. The floor in the upper half of this first hut had been slabbed. Large flat stones had been laid to create a reasonably flat surface. When excavated, it was found that some of the slabs were missing. It's reasonable to assume that they had perhaps been taken to complete or repair the floor of another hut at a later date.

It was implied by a visiting member of the Archaeological Association that the huts could have been of the 'beehive' type: that is, the roofs were formed by sloping the stonework inward as it ascended, to form a blunt cone. Although this method was used in some parts of Britain, particularly in the North, it was decided, presumably by the other members of the team or perhaps by Mr Harold Hughes himself, that the small amount of fallen stone within the huts on this site suggested otherwise.

It will be remembered that some one hundred years earlier Richard Fenton described just such a hut and implied that although it did not appear to have any aperture in the walls the roof had originally been formed by overlapping the flat stones inward slightly until they met and formed a blunt cone. In this he was quite definite. He says, 'The stonework was perfect beyond the part that had begun to contract into an arch.' He was quite certain too that the hut was seen 'at the base of the great mountain,' *during* their descent not after it. In view of this it is the author's opinion that the hut concerned was likely to have been at the base of the summit cone and not at the base of the mountain proper.

A brief aside in the description of a visit by a Mr Halliwell in 1846 again brings to notice this mode of construction. With regard to the huts he says, 'Some of them were singularly perfect, and one, near the present North West entrance to the fortress, is yet covered with a roof but we could not penetrate within, and did not feel ourselves justified in attempting to remove the stones.' Tantalisingly Mr Halliwell says stones and not roofing materials. Presumably he was referring to the stones blocking a doorway. Were the entrance blocked and the roof intact as Halliwell's remark suggests, access would automatically have been attempted through the obvious entrance. It seems unlikely that he and his companions would have attempted the dangerous business of dismantling a stone slab roof to gain entry.

In his description of the dwellings Bezant Lowe supposes that the masonry continued to overlap until it met in the centre, 'forming a circular oval shaped roof. This was no doubt overlaid with turf etc, to keep out the wind and wet, thus giving them a bee-hive appearance.' Perhaps the 'visiting member' of the Archaeological Society had a point.

The hut in question during the excavations is also at the lowest level within the walled area of the encampment. (Fig. 7)

Within this first hut twenty-seven pebbles were found. They were of various sizes with the smallest being three inches by two. One pebble was some eight inches long and had apparently been used as a rubber. Rubbers were used to smooth down leather during the tanning process, for smoothing other stones and a variety of other household activities that required a wearing down or crushing process. One of the pebbles was flat and had been rubbed to a blunt axe shape. It was about five inches long.

An animal tooth was also found, It appeared to be that of, a species of ancient shorthorn cattle. A little more enticing was a heavily corroded iron ring about a quarter of an inch thick and

BEE HIVE TYPE

PERHAPS COVERED WITH TURF

Alwyn S. Evans

fig.7

one inch in diameter. It was attached to another small piece of iron and could have been the handle from a small cauldron-like vessel. This was found in the lower of the two chambers within the hut. Another possibility is that it was part of a horse bit.

Of the pebbles found, about half had been used as rubbers or pounders and the others appeared to have been potboilers. Almost all of the items were found within 6 ins of the surface, suggesting that they might have been the possessions of the later, or even the last inhabitants. Some charcoal was found in the entrance tunnel. There is no explanation as to whether it was found on the surface or as the result of digging.

In the second hut (B on the plan) similar pebbles to those in the first hut were again found but this time there was a fragment of a much larger stone of some type of composite. It was estimated that the original stone measured some ten inches by seven inches by about four and a half inches thick. One face was worn perfectly smooth by rubbing and it was considered to be for use on a saddle quern. (Fig. 8) Shaped pebbles and stones, however fulfilling to find, cannot on their own be reliably used to date a site. They had a variety of uses through many periods in history: they are still used today in many

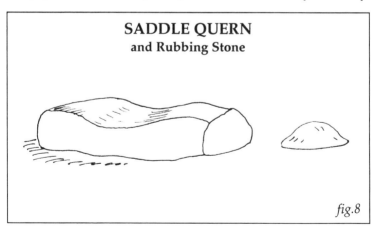

SADDLE QUERN
and Rubbing Stone

fig.8

underdeveloped countries for a variety of tasks, to rub or pound corn into flower for example.

Reward

Better was to come. What was to prove another minute step toward identifying the fort's period of use was the discovery of a bronze pin and spring of a brooch of late La Tene type. The bow of the brooch was missing. La Tene is a lake near Neuchatel in Switzerland where artefacts of this period were first found and identified in 1858. La Tene is therefore the name applied for convenience to those articles, wherever they are found, relating to the second great period of development in Celtic culture in central and Western Europe. It represents Celtic culture at the time of its maximum development from about the 5th century BC through the early years of the Roman occupation. The familiar whirls and graceful curves of Celtic design with which most people are familiar belong to this period

The third hut chosen for exploration was within the inner wall, a short distance NNE of the entrance (Marked C). This proved to be a disappointment. Other than a small fragment of charcoal, nothing was found; it was not even possible to recognise an entrance. The floor was not paved and was so destroyed that an original floor level could not be identified. It was agreed too that the hut had never even been roofed in. As time was pressing and it appeared that little would be gained from further effort, it was decided to abandon the excavation of that hut.

The next two huts to be searched and catalogued were huts D and E. Both were within the inner wall and close to it. The internal measurements of hut D were 17 ft from North to South and 15ft 6 ins from East to West. Hut E was similar in size and whereas D was seen to be round, E was quite oval in appearance. It can be seen from these measurements that the dwellings were not small but could be considered comparative to a bedroom or living room in the average modern house.

Hut D produced more clues. Once again the hut was built with its rear wall onto the sloping ground and its front facing east and slightly above ground level. The entrance was 4ft 9 ins wide. The walls in the main were still in good order and stood 4ft above the original floor level.

Within the hut some black, sticky, soil was found and this was described as having been animal matter. Whether it was thought that this was due to animals having been slaughtered and cleaned in the hut in some ancient time; or whether an animal or animals had crept in to shelter or die at some later date is not made clear. Most of the floor surface was slabbed and apart from some fallen masonry, was clear of any other deposit. In this hut were found further clues about Braich-y-Dinas.

Many pieces of broken pottery of various types were found, together with a variety of stone implements similar to those found in the earlier searches. One difference here was that one of the stones was considered to be a spindle whorl. (Fig. 9) It was about two inches in diameter and was a little over a quarter of an inch thick. It was pierced through its centre by a hole, tapering from each side suggesting that it had been worn through from each side in turn. It has been mooted on other similar sites whether these could have doubled as fishing weights. The close proximity of the sea in our case could make this believable. Four tiny fragments of an iron object were uncovered but they were so corroded that not even a sensible guess could be made. Some fragments of bones were found, the longer bones split down the middle to give access to the marrow, which was often eaten uncooked.

Hut E was not in as good condition as its neighbour. The walls were dilapidated and stood to an appreciable height in only some places. The highest part of the walls was 3ft 9ins

SPINDLE WHORL

fig.9

Alwyn S. Evans

**The Spindle Whorls differed slightly in size but
the basic design remained the same .**

above the ancient floor level. One again the entrance faced to
the East but was a little unusual in that it formed a shallow
funnel, the inner measurement being 3ft 11ins across. The outer
end was somewhat wider. The entrance was blocked by large
fallen slabs and was not cleared during the excavation.

Outside the hut and some two feet to the left was a hearth
stone, it measured 2ft 3ins by 1ft 4ins and was tilted away from
the wall. It was covered with charcoal. There was another
hearth inside the hut, four feet from the entrance. This was also
covered with charcoal and other evidence of much burning. The
soil covering the floor was only a few inches thick and did not
contain any animal fat or tissue. This dwelling contained the
usual array of pebbles of various sizes, used for rubbing,
pounding and pot boiling. In times of danger the smaller
pebbles could have doubled as sling stones. There were several
spindle whorls, all similar in size to those found previously.
There was one exception, it was a spindle whorl made of clay,

of the same diameter as the stone versions, it was twice as thick. The extra thickness was no doubt essential because of the rather delicate nature of the material used. A few bones were unearthed; one of which was quite long.

The find of real value in this hut was pottery. Smashed in the main into very tiny fragments: one or two larger pieces survived but even they were small. It was all sufficiently well preserved however for the colour and texture to be recognisable. Pottery has a distinct fingerprint and can be traced to a time and place and people by means of its shape, texture and style.

When all five plots had been searched and sieved, the evidence was forwarded to other departments for the identification of some items and the confirmation of others. The brooch pin and examples of pottery were sent to Mr C.H. Read of the British Museum. He examined them and wrote in reply, 'The relics you have sent are interesting but fragmentary. The brooch is certainly a La Tene type, maybe first or even second century BC, but it is too imperfect to say more with certainty. The dark piece of pottery with the surface rubbed is also late Celtic and more or less contemporary with the brooch. The other pottery I would have classed as Roman, first century AD.' We must ask ourselves whether these fragments of pottery and a small pin are the treasured heirlooms of a family, which handed them down from generation to generation, until they arrived on Pen-y-Dinas where they were broken and lost. Do they on they other hand tell us that our mountain top refuge was inhabited as early as two hundred years BC? Of the two I think I would feel safer with the latter.

The various bones were sent to Professor Boyd Dawkins. Sir William Boyd Dawkins 1837-1929, was a Welsh geologist. He was born at Buttington near Welshpool and was renowned in his time for his knowledge of early humans and their environs. He confirmed that the tooth found in the first hut was the lower molar of Bos Longifrons and identified the long bone as the femur of a horse.

The identification of the tooth confirmed what was already suspected, that these early people had a type of oxen which they used primarily as beasts of burden and possibly to supply milk. When the animals could no longer perform this work or could no longer be fed, they were slaughtered and the meat preserved, to be eaten later. The horse femur presents a different problem. It is well known that the Celts were horse lovers but horses were usually the possessions of the warrior or noble classes: did these rather primitive hill people have them? These questions will be approached again later when more is revealed about the environment and conditions in which the people lived.

The pottery pieces or sherds were somewhat more enlightening. They were a mixture of rough pottery and wheel turned vessels. Some appeared to have been native: the wheel turned examples were almost certainly of Roman origin. One of the bowls, of which sufficient remained to form the basis for a reconstruction (Fig. 10); and one of the vessels, had rims approximately six and a half inches in diameter: no calculation of depth seems to have been attempted. It is extremely unlikely that any of these vessels were subjected to direct heat for cooking and were used primarily for storage or as a form of eating vessel.

In his summing up, the excavation director Mr Hughes was of the opinion that the pottery found and the condition of the soil in hut D indicated that the preparing of food and its consumption took place in that hut. He thought that hut E was chiefly used for other work such as spinning and weaving

We now have a clearer idea of how these early 'Pennites' lived. We know that they had oxen- like cattle and perhaps horses as domestic animals: it's likely that these were also a source of food. We know that they used heated pebbles to heat or even boil water. The spinning whorls tell us that they wove and spun their own material, probably coarse wool. It appears

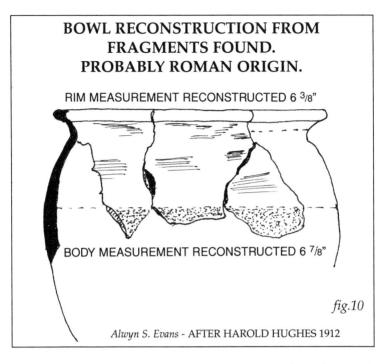

BOWL RECONSTRUCTION FROM FRAGMENTS FOUND. PROBABLY ROMAN ORIGIN.

RIM MEASUREMENT RECONSTRUCTED 6 3/8"

BODY MEASUREMENT RECONSTRUCTED 6 7/8"

fig.10

Alwyn S. Evans - AFTER HAROLD HUGHES 1912

that the resulting clothing would have been held in place with metal pins and brooches, probably of bronze or bone. They continued to use smooth stones for a variety of domestic purposes. As the excavations continued, further snippets came to light that would help to restore the picture of life on the mountaintop.

All the huts were of the same basic construction. On average they were about sixteen feet in diameter internally, their walls had been possibly five feet high and it is likely that they were crowned by a wooden framed, thatched roof. The thatch would have been whatever suitable material was to hand: in this case turf, heather, ferns and long marsh grasses. The roof could have been held in place by being attached to a wooden frame built into the walls, but is more likely to have been perched on top and held down by ropes or lengths of leather to which large stones were attached. Larger slabs could have been laid on the roof to provide extra weight. (Figs. 11-12) At such an altitude and on such an exposed slope, despite being on the lee side, it can be appreciated that holding the roof in place would have presented quite a problem. On other Iron Age sites it is suspected that wooden posts were sometimes sunk into the ground inside the walls as a further support for the roof. The rocky ground surface on Braich-y-Dinas would undoubtedly have made the latter method difficult though not impossible.

As has been suggested, not all the huts were used for the same purpose. One (Hut I) was more pear shaped than round, with its axis to the Northeast. It had a long, funnel shaped entrance, which was nine feet long, seven feet wide at its mouth and three feet four inches at the actual doorway. The walls of this hut were five to six feet thick: somewhat thicker than the average hut. Inside were found some pieces of red pottery and some pieces of handles of the same material. The handles were elongated, about four inches long, and designed to be attached vertically on a vessel which might suggest that when complete, the pot had an appreciable depth. A large lump of iron, still attached to pieces of charcoal, together with significant amounts of charcoal found in other parts of the hut could arguably attest to this hut having been the hut of a metal worker. The clay vessel had perhaps been filled with water for tempering the metal. The direction of the general construction of the hut, together with the long, funnel shaped entrance hinting that it was created in such a fashion to aid the retention of heat, could perhaps add some strength to this interpretation.

Hut J had a similar configuration and like its neighbour was smaller than the other huts. Could these two huts have been workshops?

Other huts, those with animal refuse and fats in them but little evidence of human habitation, might well have been used

130

ROOF COVERING OF MIXED MATERIALS

fig.11

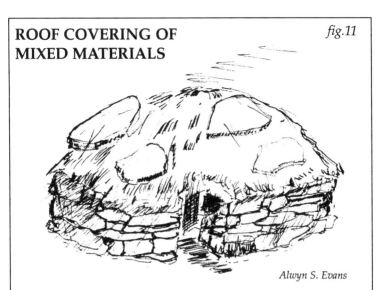

Alwyn S. Evans

THATCHED ROOF COVERING WITH PROBABLE CENTRAL POLE SUPPORT

fig.12

Alwyn S. Evans

only for the penning and slaughter of animals and the scraping and drying of hides. The treatment of hides in those days was not the tanning of later years. It consisted of laying the skin on the ground or stretching it in a wooden frame and scraping with small sharp flakes of stone until all the soft matter was completely removed. The softening process was probably rubbing with the larger smooth stones found in most of the excavated huts. It has to be constantly borne in mind that this rebuilding process is based on the remains found at Braich-y-Dinas coupled with the knowledge acquired before and since, of activities in other villages of the same period, which have produced more compelling evidence.

Several pieces of what appeared to be small sections of iron sheet found in some of the huts were considered by the team to be a mixture of ancient and modern. Those considered to be ancient were so small and corroded as to be impossible to categorise as anything other than simply pieces of metal. That is to say they had no identifiable form. As usual, the find most likely to help in the task of reconstructing life in the village was the pottery. As more and more was found, it became evident that some was of a rather primitive, native type but that the remainder, the red, wheel turned pottery, was Roman and as such, probably produced at Holt near Chester.

Vessels from the Roman potteries at Holt have been found in native settlements all over NorthWales, in hillforts and lowland farms.

Holt was established toward the end of the first century AD. It could be associated with the rebuilding in stone of the garrison at Deva (Chester) in 102 AD where roof tiles and hypocaust piping would have been needed. The site at Holt was most active in the latter part of the first century and into the first half of the second, but was not completely abandoned until the fourth century. Perhaps the most telling snippet of information is from John Wacher in 'Roman Britain'. He says of Holt, 'The kilns, eight in number, not only produced brick and tile, but also pottery, mainly of early second century types.'

Work continued on Braich-y-Dinas. The labours of the excavators were greatly assisted by the continued consent and assistance of The North Wales Granite Company, which was what the quarrying operations were now called since The Penmaenmawr Granite Quarries had amalgamated with the Welsh granite coy at Trevor on the Llŷn peninsula in 1911.

Disappointingly, the finds were, in the main, indifferent and fell within the scope and type of those found earlier. It was not until May of 1914 that finds of further interest were unearthed. It would serve no purpose to identify individually from now on, all of the huts and their contents covered in 1911 unless they were of significant value. The general size and condition of the dwellings should by now be clear but if any differences, irregularities or refinements need to be mentioned to avoid confusion, they will be included.

1914

Discoveries made in 1914 included an iron ring with an internal diameter of one and a half inches. It was riveted to another iron article but the latter was extremely corroded and could not be identified. Could it have been the remains of another cauldron? Readers of Celtic history will realise how often cauldrons are mentioned and what an important item they were in domestic life. The excavation team considered that insufficient remained for any calculated guess to be made as to its use: the guess as to its possible identity is mine.

Of interest was the head and upper stem of a large iron nail; the head was estimated to have been a little under an inch across and the stem about half that in diameter and some two inches long. Whether it was of local or Roman origin would be hard to determine as by now no doubt the village smith would have been adept at copying the simpler Roman items. Further investigation brought to light dozens of spindle whorls. These varied in standard and conveyed several different degrees of workmanship. Such a large number of whorls suggests that spinning played a major part in the life of the village and hints at a good supply of wool. An axe shaped stone was found. It was about four and a half inches long and had been rubbed rather than chipped to a blunt edge.

It was when the team reached a hut registered as hut T that some finds of real interest were made. A long iron object was uncovered. When it was picked up it came apart but was successfully reassembled. It was fourteen and a half inches long but it was the opinion of those present that when in its original state it could have been longer. The object was slightly curved, it was agreed however that this was probably as the result of burial and decomposition rather than deliberate shaping. An extract from the excavation report reads as follows. 'The general shape is suggestive of a dagger or a kind of knife, but the thickness of the lower portion, about 5/16 ins, which would answer to the blade, appears excessive. If the blade was contained in a metal sheath . . . the two may have combined and become one mass.'

A second find from the same hut is also worthy of mention. The report describes it thus. 'A fine quartz pebble . . . about three and a half inches in diameter, bearing a remarkable resemblance to a human head. On several faces the pebble has been rubbed down. The hollow eyes are in positions naturally occupied by crystals. It would appear that the natural resemblance to a head has been increased artificially and intentionally.' The early Celts, up to and including the Roman occupation, revered the cult of the head and sometimes took the heads of defeated enemies, displaying their trophies on their huts and making false heads of stone or wood for their religious monuments. The resemblance of this stone in its rough form to a human head probably recalled more valiant days and invited its development.

Most of the finds were now of the same nature as those found since the inspection of the huts began. Pebbles of various sizes, showing various degrees of having been shaped, ranging from a little over an inch to thirteen inches long. Animal bones and teeth, charcoal and pieces of corroded metal were all inspected, identified and catalogued. Of interest among these were the remains of a brooch and some pieces of what appeared to have been armlets or torques. The identified remains of some boar bones (Sus Scrofa) were useful: they enabled boar/pig to be added to the list of domestic animals kept. There is always the possibility of course that the boar was caught during the course of a hunt. Boar hunts feature largely in Celtic literature. The 'Twrch Trwyth' of the Mabinogion is probably the most familiar. Did wild boar roam in the oak woods which probably covered much of the lower slopes at that time?

Most and probably all of the metal finds were thought to be Roman. Those remnants of the mixtures of earth, charcoal and iron lumps could be seen as a primitive attempt by the inhabitants to create their own iron implements, albeit with very limited success. It would be dangerous nevertheless to assume that they were all unsuccessful, based on such flimsy evidence.

Something that deserves individual discussion is a piece of glass found in hut R. No measurements are given in the excavation reports therefore we have no way of determining its size. It is likely however to have been quite small. It was sent to Professor Bosanquet, who examined it and wrote, 'The glass is, I think, certainly a piece of Roman window glass. It has the characteristic of two faces, one smooth, one rough and the rounded edge. I suppose it is conceivable that some resident on Penmaenmawr indulged in the luxury of a pane or two of glass in the second or third century. But there is another possibility. I once saw on the Roman Wall a piece of glass that seemed to have been chipped into a rough arrowhead. A native might have brought this fragment away from a Roman settlement with an eye to some such use, or even as a curiosity'. Based on what had already been found and the conditions suggested in the huts, I would be inclined to go with the second possibility.

The work for the seasons 1913/14 now came to an end. Mr Harold Hughes paid particular tribute to Mr H.L. North of Llanfairfechan for his valuable help in carrying out the survey and excavations. The rough terrain, mist, rain and constant cold winds had made the labours particularly arduous. Greater trials were ahead, against which the endeavours of the excavators would seem as child's play. Europe was lurching toward the opening phases of the First World War.

No serious work was done during the war as the whole of the national effort was geared to winning that conflict. Many of the quarry workers fought in the trenches of the western front and in Gallipoli, Palestine and the Mesopotamian campaigns. The man power situation in the quarries became so critical that in nineteen seventeen, German prisoners of war were drafted in to help. They were quartered in Graiglwyd Hall: then an empty country house, currently a caravan park. To improve their route from camp to quarry they cut a path across the ffridd, thus adding yet another scar to the face of the mountain. The path is now all but grown over but is still referred to locally as 'German road'

In 1920 surveying continued but post war normality was slow to return and funds were restricted. Excavation did not resume until September 1921. During that time Mr Hughes was ably assisted by Mr Ivor E. Davies of Penmaenmawr. Mr Davies was not only very familiar with the mountain, and a particularly competent local historian but was also an employee of the Granite Company from 1907 to 1948. It was to prove a fortunate and productive partnership.

Once again the Penmaenmawr and North Wales Granite Coy. were most helpful and renewed their consent. At first, only the usual assortment of pebbles and bones were found and it must have appeared that this was now to be the general run of things.

Spirits were lifted however when a dwelling designated Hut 'Y' was reached. The excavations in this hut produced a bracelet, in the form of a coiled snake, which appeared to be made of silver, and an iron bar about 14 inches long. Although described as a bracelet, the silver item had an internal diameter of 1 7/16 inches by 1 13/16 inches. This would make it a very small bracelet, perhaps that of a child? (Fig. 13)

The item was forwarded to Dr Mortimer Wheeler (1890 – 1976), who at that time was the director of the National Museum of Wales. He reported as follows. 'The bracelet is most

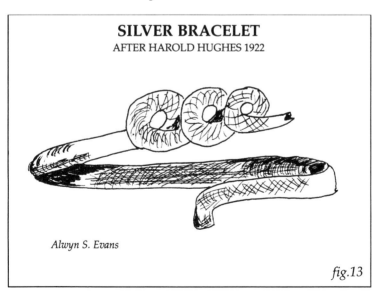

SILVER BRACELET
AFTER HAROLD HUGHES 1922

Alwyn S. Evans

fig.13

interesting. Professor W. Gowland FRS, to whom I have shown it, confirms my opinion that it is silver, partially converted into silver chloride as a result of burial in the ground. The type is a variant of one which seems to have enjoyed some popularity in Romano-British times. The bracelet is apparently intended to represent a convoluted snake, although the head is unfortunately missing . . . It may be suggested that the snake was regarded with favour by reason of its association with healing and kindred ideas.' Dr Wheeler then went on to compare the bracelet with others of a similar nature which had been found at various points in Britain, all with some Roman connection. Not all were made of silver, some were of lead or bronze. The bracelet's obvious monetary and perhaps social value would make it likely to have been the property of a person of rank. How very tempting to attempt to identify ownership; a chieftain perhaps or his wife or child? Tempting perhaps, but without *any* knowledge of the inhabitants, such an attempt would be futile.

The other significant find in this hut was an iron bar approximately 14 inches long. Another piece of iron was nearby; if the two were originally one as was mooted at the time of discovery, then the bar would have been 18 inches long. The iron bars are interesting in that they were used as currency in earlier Celtic times; and not only by Celts but by the Greeks and other early civilisations. They were considered of value, particularly by the less developed societies who could not produce their own iron because they could either be kept in the original form as currency with which to conduct further transactions at a later date or beaten into a sword blade; they were already a convenient size and shape. If they were still being used by the inhabitants of Braich-y-Dinas, as would appear to have been the case, then that would suggest that they were still retaining habits and customs abandoned by other Celtic societies long before.

Another item of interest was found, this time in Hut Z; a

shaped pebble, just a little over two and a half inches long which had been hollowed out as if designed to contain oil or some other substance, perhaps as a lamp. Several stones of similar size and worked with an identical design, were found at Tŷ Mawr on Holyhead island during the exploration there by the Hon. W.O. Stanley some years previously.

An interesting letter dated May 29, 1911, on Penmaenmawr and Welsh Granite Company head office paper, was addressed to a J. Arthur Acton of Wrexham. It was signed by Colonel A.E. Johnson. Colonel Johnson had come to the firm in 1908 as manager and retired in 1925. The letter mentions a find similar in design to the Holyhead stone but much larger. It had been found in the tumbledown wall of the encampment. The object was 10 inches in diameter and about 3 inches deep. It was hollowed out to a depth of ¼ of an inch and eight inches across. There was a small opening fashioned into its rim. The material was sandstone and according to the letter writer was not thought to have been local.

Col. Johnson was of the opinion that it could have been a kind of corn mill or quern. The description certainly fits such a use. If that is the case then it is more likely to have been of Roman than native origin. It was far removed in design and operation from the saddle querns found in and normally associated with, the hill forts of North Wales. The sandstone from which it was made might also imply that it was perhaps made in the Chester area, a sandstone district and the Roman military headquarters in North Wales. Strangely, it was not mentioned in the excavation reports.

The description and accompanying diagram in the letter suggested that it was not complete. It would, as the Colonel guessed, fit the description of having been the lower half of a rather advanced design of a corn-grinding mill, probably Roman. The movable top half would have fitted into the lower and could have been fitted with a handle to enable it to be turned. The ground flour would then have been released through the small mouth cut into one side of the bottom half. No mention is made of this implement in any of Mr Hughes's reports and it is possible that it was never reported as having been found. It could give another twist to the puzzle of who was in Braich-y-Dinas. Had it once been used by a small Roman detachment, perhaps on lookout duty on the mountaintop and living with the inhabitants? (Fig. 14)

Conflictingly, the item has also been described as a mould for making large discs. This latter description could explain the shallow hollow section and perhaps the absence of a shaped top. If it is accepted as a mould then perhaps it was native and not Roman after all.

As the excavations progressed, further finds of interest were made. Two armlets were discovered, in two separate huts. What makes them worthy of discussion is that they were made from a highly combustible bituminous stone. The material was not available locally and it was the opinion of Dr F.J. North that it was what is known as 'Kimmeridge Clay'. The Kimmeridge Clay outcrop after which the object is named occurs in Dorset, with another similar outcrop of slightly lighter coloured stone in Yorkshire. Since the excavations, other outcrops have been identified and are now thought to have been widely quarried.

Although considered to be in the non-precious section of Roman jewellery, it would almost certainly register very favourably in a rather backward hill fort on the fringe of the imperial Roman world. The arrival in Penmaenmawr of an armlet made of the substance must therefore be worthy of some contemplation. Assuming it was made in Yorkshire, how would the armlet have reached Braich-y-Dinas? The sea traffic between the west coast of northern Britain and north Wales was well established. A visiting chieftain perhaps? Was it a gift from an ally? Perhaps an auxiliary Roman soldier bought it or traded for it in Yorkshire and presented it to someone at Penmaenmawr. We can guess forever, we will never know. However it made its way here, the fact remains that it was a

PLAN OF BRAICH-Y-DINAS - 1923
ON COMPLETION OF MAIN EXCAVATION

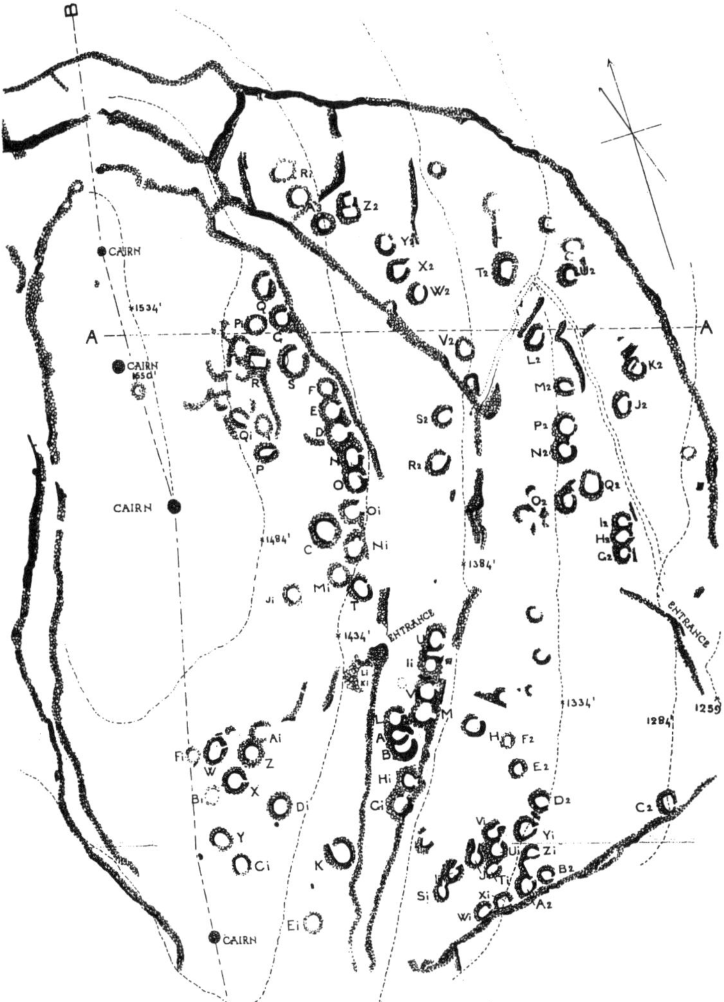

Kind permission of Archaeologia Cambrensis

fig.14

relatively expensive gift or a purchase made many miles away and it was found at Braich-y-Dinas.

It is interesting to see how these armlets were made and to consider how long the manufacture might have taken. They were made in one piece and from solid rock: because the material was combustible and therefore likely to molecular change if exposed to any appreciable heat, it is unlikely to have been subjected to any process other than carving.

It is thought that the dark, oily shale, once quarried was taken to a convenient place to be worked. Sir Mortimer Wheeler suggested at the time that the slabs were pierced and carried on a pole for convenience. The process of shaping would then begin. Using flint knives or chisel shaped stones, the worker would cut out a rough circle of appropriate size, then pierce it, using a hard stone in a drilling motion. Hammering action would almost certainly have cracked it. Finally it would be honed and rubbed to shape using abrasives, probably sandstone or some other grit, perhaps together with water. How long this process must have taken can only be guessed at. A recent book (1996) by Catherine Johns states that circular bangles could have been produced on a primitive lathe. Whether this reduced their value, as they might then have become more plentiful is hard to say. Perhaps their value was held constant by the very mechanics and technique required for their production.

However they were made, the fact that the articles had travelled some considerable distance meant that they are not likely to have been worn by all and sundry: could they have been the prized possessions of some minor chieftain? That they would have held high value in such a community is undeniable. Once again the source could have been Roman. (Fig. 15)

Other finds of note were brought to light. A certain amount of cautious excitement must have been felt when a mass of iron with fragments of charcoal attached was found. Interest in this

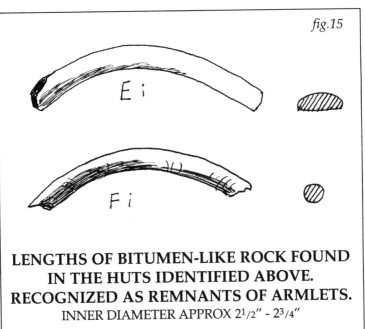

fig.15

E i

F i

LENGTHS OF BITUMEN-LIKE ROCK FOUND IN THE HUTS IDENTIFIED ABOVE. RECOGNIZED AS REMNANTS OF ARMLETS.

INNER DIAMETER APPROX $2^1/2''$ - $2^3/4''$

Alwyn S. Evans - AFTER HAROLD HUGHES

dissolved rather quickly however when Dr North stated that it in his opinion the iron was corroded not smelted and that the charcoal attached to it was the result of close contact over many years and not the outcome of some process of manufacture. As if to compensate for this disappointment, further iron objects were found which were to shed a little more light on the lifestyle of the village people.

An iron implement nearly eleven inches long was thought to have been a gouge; and several pieces of pointed metal were considered as almost certainly the remains of weapons. They bore a resemblance to the butt ends of spears. (Fig. 16) Another iron nail was also found. In the same hut as the iron implements and weapons there was a well-formed hearth which appeared to be partly built into the wall. In the hut, but not, it appears, in the hearth: there was a mass of material, parts of which had a highly glazed surface. Dr North wrote of this, 'These fragments contain silica, alumina and other substances usually found in slags from metallic ores, such as those of lead or zinc. There is no metallic matter remaining to indicate the nature of the ore, but it is not likely to have been iron or copper.' What then was the mass of glazed material? It had obviously been subjected to intense heat, but where? There was a hearth in the hut but nothing to suggest that the heat had been created there.

It was already recognised that the villagers had knowledge of primitive smelting but nothing was found to imply that they were capable of creating and sustaining the sort of fierce and

IRON IMPLEMENT 11" LONG - GOUGE? WEAPON?

SPEAR BUTT

Alwyn S. Evans - AFTER HAROLD HUGHES   *fig.16*

sustained temperatures required in creating the glazed mass. Was it a find, picked up somewhere unrelated to the village and the hut, which had appealed to a primitive mind and was brought home as a curio? It seems unlikely. Perhaps the refuse tips of Caerhun Roman fort were again the source. Repairs to sea going Roman supply vessels were undertaken there and could presumably have produced this sort of residue.

Recent (that is within the last five years) experiments designed to recreate the heat required for successful ore smelting and high grade metal work under iron age conditions and using the methods and equipment of the period, proved beset by problems. It took many hours to reach the required heat and severe loss was experienced when the forge was opened, however briefly, to add ore. More hours of pumping air through the fire was then needed to reach the optimum temperature once more. The air was forced through the fire by means of bellows made of wood and animal skin. The actual metal working process proved more successful but was no less arduous. These experiments were undertaken by different groups of academics and craftsmen in England while trying to recreate Iron Age villages. They were carefully conducted under strict conditions.

When the searchers reached a hut designated Ji, There were signs of a fire in the middle. That was not unusual, but what was also found gave an uncertain clue to the as yet incompletely recognised capabilities of the occupants. A lump of decomposed mineral substance recovered from the hut was submitted to Dr North for his opinion and this is what he had to say. 'This is a nearly completely decomposed fragment of Galena (lead sulphite). Portions of the grey galena remain but the bulk of the specimen is now lead sulphide. This may be due either to natural weathering, or the specimen having been burnt in a current of air' (in a furnace?).

This opinion was helpful in some respects but added in other ways to the ambiguity about the capabilities of the villagers. It does reinforce the idea that some of the huts were or could have been used purely for the smelting and working of iron. Again we are faced with the puzzle that our villagers might have had had the technology to create heat of the degree required to produce iron and the resulting artefacts and yet remain dependent in the main on stone implements and metal ware scrounged from the Roman garrisons. Why? Perhaps they could create the heat but did not have access to the ore in any great quantity. Was the air current referred to by Dr North created not by the inhabitants of Pen-y-Dinas but by the military in the valleys below? It is now virtually impossible to be sure and all we can do is add the conundrum to the considerable list of mysteries associated with the vanished village.

As the late autumn weather closed in bringing with it the damp clinging mountain mists, work on the site drew to a close. 1921 had been perhaps a little more productive than the previous years. More pieces of metal had been found and the indications of smelting, and its associated puzzles, had given food for thought. The general feeling was that the fort or fortified village had not been occupied earlier or much later than the Roman occupation of the country, that is from the late first to the early fifth century AD. Even the La Tene style brooch found in 1911 was now thought to have been a copy of Roman origin. Of all the items found to date, the only objects of local manufacture were thought to be those made of stone. It was becoming obvious that the culture here on the mountain was appreciably less advanced than that in the southern and more fertile half of Britain.

1922

1922 opened with a grant of fifty pounds made by The Board of Celtic Studies: generous by the values of the day. Invaluable assistance came also in the form of Mr Goronwy ap Griffith who camped out on the mountain for the duration of the excavations. This gentleman was also generous enough to give of his time to help in measuring the site and the hutments. Thanks was also due to Messrs. Ivor E. Davies, Arthur E. Elias and Perris Elias who contributed considerably to the success of the operations. Two students from the University College at Bangor also devoted two days each to the proceedings.

The extra manpower made a considerable difference. During that season thirty-five huts were excavated. Most revealed the now standard fare of pebbles, fire ash and bits of assorted bone. This was to be expected however and was offset by the discovery of some further worthwhile items and variations in hut design. Some huts showed no sign at all of occupation at any time and others were obviously unfinished. Were these huts destined for occupation by some additions to the village population or was it simply expedient to move to new quarters when some of the older ones became uninhabitable? Nothing is known of the sanitary arrangements or even whether they existed at all. It is easy to imagine that after several, perhaps many years of occupation, conditions in the huts must have deteriorated considerably and become quite foul.

Hut Ui was unusual in that, apart from the customary fire in the centre of the hut, a stone ledge was built into the far wall opposite the entrance. This ledge took up about a quarter of the floor space. Was it a form of sleeping ledge perhaps, or food storage?

Several of the dwellings had roughly paved floors. One or two were double huts with the remains of fire in one section but not the other, nothing was found however to indicate why they had been built in this fashion. Mr Hughes deliberately emphasised here that where fire is mentioned during excavation, it indicates much burning and not simply odd bits of burned wood or charcoal here and there.

This period of the dig exposed considerably more pottery

pieces, nearly all were considered to have been from the early first to the mid second century AD. Some of the pieces were identified as having been Samian Ware. Perhaps the most interesting pieces of pottery were those that were found in hut T2.

135 pieces of amphorae, some buff coloured and others a dull red, indicated that they had found the remains of more than one type of vessel. Using the curvature of the remaining fragments as a guide, it was determined that they would have had a diameter of 20 to 21 inches.

The Roman army used amphorae to transport wine and olive oil, fish paste, dates and so forth from the Mediterranean to their outlying forts. The containers varied in design but the two most familiar were those of a globular shape with a flat bottom and others of an almost carrot shape. The latter were about three feet high, usually with two elongated handles and a tapered base. Both types had long, rather delicate necks. The flat-bottomed variety was stored in the ordinary way, by simply standing on a floor or shelf.

The long carrot shaped ones were used to carry bulk stores on board ships. Their design was such that they could be held upright in a hole and so were secure against the rocking of the vessel when at sea. They could be found stacked in rows of hundreds in racks in the ships that re supplied the forts like Kanovium (Caerhun), and Segontium (Caernarfon). Once out of the ship's storage racks, they were difficult to store upright and unless re-seated in similar racks in the quartermaster's store, were easily broken: the necks were particularly vulnerable. When that happened they were discarded.

It is almost certain that the fragments found at Braich-y-Dinas were the lower remains of a variety of broken but still usable containers scrounged from the rubbish tips of the forts. The scenes at some of the garrisons must have been reminiscent of those at the military outposts during the western expansion in America, as native Americans scrounged amongst the waste tips looking for useable bits and pieces.

It is likely that the villagers would have found the flat-bottomed variety of amphora most convenient for domestic use. The ones with the pointed base could conceivably have been held upright in shallow holes or supported between stones and used for some commodity, access to which did not require constant upending of the vessel. In the absence of storage pits perhaps these amphorae were used for storing a day's supply of water or surplus corn and seed.

More iron rings were found and judging by the angle at which the remnants of pieces of corroded metal were attached to them, they appeared to have been pot handles; perhaps cooking pots. These later digs unearthed more clues to the villagers' diet. The discovery of limpet, mussel, cockle and periwinkle shells were evidence that shellfish figured in the culinary composition. No doubt the close proximity of the seashore would have made this inevitable.

One or two of the huts had small pieces of coal in their hearths. This was something of a deviation from the usual wood or peat and although Dr North was sure that it was from a North Wales field he was unwilling to attempt to pinpoint the source. Bituminous, shale coal lies fairly close to the surface and is revealed from time to time as the result of a flood or small landslide. It is also commonly found washed up on the beach when it is known as sea coal. As earlier evidence suggested that the villagers visited the beach for food and perhaps to fish, maybe that is where they found it.

The huts searched during this season revealed more evidence of visits to the local garrisons. Small beads of coloured glass similar to those favoured by Roman women and often found in Roman forts and settlements were uncovered by the searchers.

During this period of excavation the spirits of the excavators, which by now could have been understandably jaded, were given a welcome boost. Coins began to appear. The discovery of Roman coins among the detritus was a much needed bench mark on which to establish and stabilise dates. The coins also provided further evidence of contact between the garrisons and the hillforts. The possible reasons for this contact are too numerous to be covered here but are debated in some detail in the closing discussion. A list of the coins found during the whole of the operations on the mountain can be found in index No. 1.

Hut Zi produced an iron ring, which was considered to have been a chain link. By comparing it with the scale provided by Mr Hughes in his report, it appears to have been approximately two inches long and one and a half inches wide. The circumference of the metal is difficult to judge because of the swelling action of the layers of corrosion but appears to have been about half an inch. If a use for the chain was guessed at then there are several possibilities. Was it of Roman manufacture? If so, it was probably a short length lifted from a dump at a military camp and used for suspending one of the cauldrons mentioned earlier over a cooking fire. If it were of native manufacture then it could have been put to an altogether more sinister use.

Slavery

The Celts were slaveholders and in earlier times, before the Roman invasion, slaves, hunting dogs, hides and tin were some of Britain's main exports to the continent. The Roman historian Strabo commented in the first century AD that one of the attractions of Britain was the large number of slaves that could be obtained. Although many of the slaves he mentions were undoubtedly prisoners as the result of Roman military campaigns: in earlier times unrest and warfare between the native tribes had provided thousands more.

In 1943, during the extension of the runways at RAF Valley on Anglesey a slave chain was found in a marshy area known as Llyn Cerrig Bach. It was several yards long and consisted of a chain interspersed with neck links. For some days it was used for towing heavy plant and vehicles in the muddy conditions. It was only when the chain was recognised for what it was that he practice ceased. The chain was none the worse for its mishandling which gives some idea of its strength. It was thought to have been thrown into a pond as a votive offering, possibly shortly before the Roman invasion of Anglesey in 59 AD. To what extent the inhabitants of Braich-y-Dinas held slaves is debatable: presumably very few and possibly none at all.

Hut U2 produced an interesting stone. It was a type of grit and had been worked by hand to produce what appear to be finger grips from its apex to its rim and a shallow groove around the circumference a little below the rim. The stone was in form and size similar to half a grapefruit. The flat surface was slightly concave and rough, giving a good grinding surface: it appeared to have been the lower half of a hand held quern and was thought to have been used for grinding small quantities of a substance: possibly pigments or perhaps herbs. There was a small lip, apparently for the discharge of the ground substance.

Mr Jones, who lived in the house called Pen-y-Penmaen, which was on the Eastern, that is the Penmaenmawr side, just outside the lower wall, made an accidental find during this time. He was removing stone for wall repair from the mass of scree outside the limits of the excavated area when he came across a circular stone approximately four and a half inches in diameter. It was about threequarters of an inch thick and pierced in the centre. Although the stone had sustained considerable damage, the remaining undamaged surfaces were polished. No comment was made about its possible use.

Some slag found in one of the huts was sent to Dr North at

the National Museum and this is what he had to say about it. 'The slag contains a good deal of iron and some sulphur, and a trace of phosphorous. It presumably represents an iron ore of the Haematite type rather than the clay-iron stone type. There is a considerable amount of metal still remaining in it. There are several iron ore deposits in North Wales and Cumberland from which such an ore could have been obtained.' It should be pointed out again that to produce the iron and the slag deposit, a temperature of 1000 degrees centigrade was required and had to be sustained for a considerable time, perhaps several hours. No mean feat with a home made smelting oven made of a kind of firebrick made of clay. (Fig. 17)

A find that remains a complete mystery was some dust, which was discovered under the northern edge of the summit cairn. It was submitted to Dr R.E. Mortimer Wheeler. His response was that it contained bone dust but that nothing else could be said about it. Would the people of Braich-y-Dinas have taken the trouble to inter the bones of an animal under the cairn

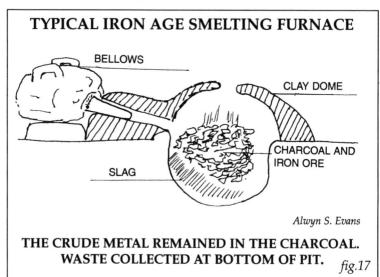

TYPICAL IRON AGE SMELTING FURNACE

BELLOWS

CLAY DOME

CHARCOAL AND IRON ORE

SLAG

Alwyn S. Evans

THE CRUDE METAL REMAINED IN THE CHARCOAL. WASTE COLLECTED AT BOTTOM OF PIT. *fig.17*

on the topmost ridge of the mountain? Probably not: could it have been human, perhaps some long dead chieftain or village headman? We will never know.

During this season of excavation the team ranged slightly further afield and explored several cairns some one hundred and fifty yards or so to the east of the mountain, on flat ground described as fields in their reports. The cairns were about twenty feet in diameter and carefully made from piled stones with soil heaped over them although this was much weathered by time, wind and rain. The barrows, for that is what they turned out to be, were thought in all probability to have been the burial places of the inhabitants of the village: or perhaps only the most important. Although considerable time and effort was spent on exploring these burial places, no bones were found.

As the excavations progressed another accidental find was made. Mr Ivor Davies was given a piece of porringer, a shallow clay dish common during the Roman occupation. It had been found, not on the mountaintop by an archaeologist, but by a farmer while burying a dead sheep in some swampy ground to the west of Graiglwyd Hall over a mile away and some 1200 feet lower. The vessel fragment was of a polished black ware outside and light grey inside. When he was shown the vessel, Mr Harold Hughes voiced some surprise that a find of that kind and dating from the same period as those pieces found within the area of excavation had been made at such a low level. Both he and Mr Davies made a thorough search of the area but could find no evidence to suggest ancient human habitation.

Upon closer examination of the pottery, it was agreed that the dish, when complete would have had an outside diameter of seven and one eighth inches. A scale drawing was made of the porringer and sent to Dr Wheeler. He wrote, 'The porringer is of a type which cannot be dated with any precision. It seems to have run on with very little variation through the Roman period. The earlier types (pre Antonine) generally have a chamfer between side and base, and the absence of this feature from the Graiglwyd specimen suggests that it is not notably early. On the other hand, it might be of any date from mid second to fourth century.' (Fig. 18)

Time and finance were now against the searchers. The site was becoming progressively isolated among the quarry works and little had come to light to suggest that further work would produce knowledge to surpass that already gained. It is probable too that it would have been difficult to qualify further expense on a site that was unlikely to give up anything of quantifiable value. Those items that had been found were catalogued, indexed and safely deposited, mainly with the national Museum of Wales.

That season of 1922 was the last when any serious planned inspection of the inner site was made. All identifiable traces outside the main walled area were examined and where feasible, excavated. They produced nothing of any significance. Those items found as the result of that brief excavation are now also in the National Museum of Wales, Cardiff. The quarrying

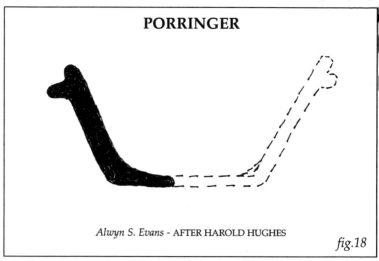

PORRINGER

Alwyn S. Evans - AFTER HAROLD HUGHES

fig.18

continued and all evidence of any ancient habitation eventually vanished in to the great maws of the crushers.

Discussion

The collecting of evidence is relatively straightforward when compared to what is done with that evidence once it has been gathered. How easy it would be to look at the obvious clues and say 'Right, this is what happened or this is who they were, here is where they came from or that is where they went.' Such an approach is dangerously simplistic and with the limited knowledge available to us about the inhabitants of Braich-y-Dinas, the result would almost certainly be wrong.

This discussion is aimed at trying to put together the bits and pieces, to provide a picture, albeit faint and cloudy, of what life in the village might have been like. It's done in the full knowledge that what will result is not going to be one simple, clear picture but a confusion of scenes. Some of the reconstruction will be relatively straightforward and easy to accept, other parts are likely to be quite fragmented and will assuredly raise doubts and questions. If that is the case and I have caused the reader to think about and discuss the ancient history of Penmaenmawr, then my short work has partially succeeded in its aim.

The suggestions which follow are those which have either occurred to me over the years or have been put to me during conversations with various people. Some are the result of hints provided by a variety of learned historians, in many books on the subject of the different ages of humankind and its development. Much has been gleaned from writings on the tactics and habits of the Roman army of occupation. None is put forward as being exactly what took place on Penmaenmawr although any or all of the situations and conditions described could have existed.

The most important clues to help us recreate the lives of those distant people have been provided by the records of the excavations of Braich-y-Dinas in the early part of the century by that small band of dedicated historians, amateur and professional: local and international.

Over a period of some four hundred years before the dig, a number of professional, semi- professional and rank amateur historians and even the odd poet and artist have left written accounts of their visits to the site. Of these accounts, some of the more imaginative have been responsible for providing some romantic and often confusing impressions, misconceptions and fanciful stories.

Going back over the years to the late sixteenth century, these early reports, although in some cases clearly exaggerated, should not be dismissed as irrelevant. They are based on what those early explorers **saw** and that is clearly very different from what was to be seen years later in the twentieth century. Events such as the laws of land enclosure, which appeared to give licence to desk bound urban clerks to draw arbitrary lines across the countryside, tempted the builders of the resulting requirement for miles of dry stone walling to cause extensive damage to the village in their search for easily available raw material. Arch Deacon Evans said in 1803 that, for example, most of the stones from the carneddau, from which the mountain range took its name, were removed for wall building to satisfy an enclosure act.

The perimeter walls of the village witnessed by those early explorers in the sixteen hundreds would for instance have been considerably higher and the huts roofless but much more distinct than those in the nineteen hundreds. Before the walls were torn down and the resultant rubble strewn about, the pathways would have been clearly marked and the entrance or entrances distinct. With this in mind perhaps the pictures painted by the early reports are more accurate than we with our twenty first century overconfidence might be willing to accept.

Mention is made in some of those early accounts of towers or the bases of towers. Some early settlements in Scotland, similar to though smaller than the one on Penmaenmawr, do have towers. These are Brochs and are a Pictish design: may we suppose that it is possible that sixteenth century reporters mistook those remains on Braich-y-Dinas for something akin to the brochs but in greater numbers? Although it is unlikely that the huts were ever intended to be such, the closeness or even attachment of some of to the perimeter walls could have made the idea of towers seem feasible at the time.

Visitors to Tre'r Ceiri near Llanaelhaearn in Gwynedd will still be able to see perimeter walls surrounding a settlement very similar in design and of the same period as Braich-y-Dinas. The walls there are still extant to a height of some eight or nine feet on their outer sides.

The early twentieth century excavation reports are, as one might expect, precise and scientific. They record what was found and that is all: where opinions are offered, they are brief and non-committal.

Although we might be able to work out what the villagers ate and wore and how long they might have lived, the one question that cannot be addressed with any certainty is **who** they were.

Let's consider what we have. We know that many thousands of years ago there were people making stone implements and living on the ridge above Penmaenmawr. Hut platforms, hut circles, track remains, field patterns, traces of fire and charcoal and standing stones all tell of their presence. We are not sure where the earliest came from or who they were. We have no clear evidence to tell us whether they lived here permanently or not; neither do we have any indication of numbers.

The evidence of Y Meini Hirion and Braich-y-Dinas tell of a

later society. When one then considers the man, and womanpower, required to erect standing stones or build a fortified village and look after animals and children, to plough, seed and harvest the fields and compares them with the scattering of dwellings that cover the hills from the coast and into the Conwy valley, it allows us, with some degree of safety, to surmise that at one time the upland population must have been quite considerable.

Not only the hills but the lower reaches were farmed. Clearings were hacked out and crops planted. Traces of circular huts and at least two burial mounds have been found on the lower slopes and right down into the fields near Tŷ Mawr farm. Two of the mounds near Tŷ Mawr proved to be Bronze Age and when opened were found to contain many cinerary urns. These are the only ones recorded; others have undoubtedly been obliterated under early quarrying spoil or during medieval attempts at forest clearance and ploughing.

Early beginnings at Braich-y-Dinas

Let us suppose for a moment that perhaps as early as the second millennium BC, for some reason, perhaps family feuding, the summit of Braich-y-Dinas, like others in the area such as Alltwen overlooking the Sychnant Pass, already had a small compound on it for use in times of danger. What was to prevent these rather primitive hill people from developing that already existing compound or animal enclosure to its later size and stature as circumstances became increasingly unsettled and populations grew?

Most modern, that is twentieth century references to the settlement all maintain that the main period of habitation in the village was during the Roman occupation. That opinion is based on the dateable artefacts found there during the excavations of 1911-1922. Items manufactured from clay, metal or glass such as those uncovered by the excavations can be dated with some certainty but what of the stone implements?

The vast majority of the tools and domestic articles found were made of stone: the saddle querns and pounders for instance. Many would be damaged through use in the early days and discarded. The hard, stony surface of the mountain is unlikely to have allowed them to sink very far. Repeated building or repair of the huts could have covered them but, during the excavations, could they have reappeared? The design of the pounders and scrapers found during the excavations had changed little if at all from those used by the axe makers many thousands of years before. Items like the querns or the hammer stones would eventually be rubbed and hammered to the point where they would become useless and then be thrown away and spindle whorls be lost. They would have been buried over time, together with similar articles from the same level but from a much later age. How are we to differentiate between those made in 50 AD and those fashioned in the same way very much earlier?

Would it be far fetched to consider that the people, whatever their origin who chipped the stone axes, were not seasonal visitors but stayed in and around the locality as was supposed at the start of this tale and that it was their descendants, maybe influenced or led by, later more sophisticated newcomers who erected the stone circle and extended and lived in the hill fort altering and adapting it to suit their changing needs? Although thousands of years and several folk incursions separate them, can we with any safety say that, despite centuries of assimilation and the infusion of new blood, the stone chippers and the village dwellers remained basically the same people?

It is possible that the previous, stone working generations were not 'Celts' as we understand the word but an earlier native people who were later conquered or assimilated by early metal using Celtic refugees from further south with a superior standard of life. The newcomers in turn having been obliged to move from their tribal homelands by still further tribal movement from Gaul where the Gaulish Celts were under pressure from Rome.

Tribal movement and resettlement, either by common consent or by force of arms was commonplace at that time. Strabo c. 60 BC to 20 AD, a Greek geographer, stoic and Roman military historian, said this of the Celts, 'They are wont to change their abode on slight provocation, migrating in bands with all their battle array, or rather setting out with their households when displaced by a stronger enemy.' Could it be that our stone chippers and their henge-building descendants, if that is what they were, were 'displaced by a stronger enemy?' If so, who was the enemy? Superior Bronze Age or iron age Celts? They would have been unlikely to have abandoned prosperous lowland farmsteads to come here unless for gain or if under extreme pressure. We have no way of telling whether, when they did arrive they exterminated the existing population or whether they simply killed the men and used the women and children as slaves. Perhaps they did neither. Did *they* build the village on Braich-y-Dinas?

It surely stretches credibility to believe, as some explanations for the settlement suggest, that a band of people suddenly turned up for no recorded reason, ousted the indigenous population if there was one, built the settlement and vanished again some three or four hundred years later without leaving any clue as to their identity or where or why they went. I submit it is more likely that a gradual evolution took place; an evolution that only ceased when the need to live under such conditions no longer existed or when the uplands would no longer support the people and they were obliged to disperse to survive.

The one aspect of this history that can be approached with any confidence of accuracy is the lifestyle of the inhabitants of Braich-y-Dinas. The painstaking excavations revealed much that could be used to provide at least a general overview.

161

Food

Corn grinding querns showed that they had sufficient cereal to produce flour for bread. The oats, spelt wheat and barley was probably grown on the lower, more sheltered slopes, to the South and Southwest which had a longer exposure to the sun. The advent of winter sown wheat meant that if all went according to plan, they could look forward to two crops in a growing year. Greens could have been raised on the less sunny slopes to the east. Evidence of stone clearing to create fields was discovered outside the limit of the outer defensive wall in the late nineteen forties and early fifties.

Other, usually more prosperous lowland sites have produced pieces of simple Bronze Age ploughs known as ards. Made predominantly of wood, they sometimes had metal tips to the blade to enable the working of newer, rougher pastures as well as established fields. By the time of the late Iron Age

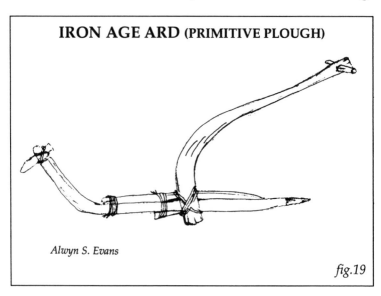

IRON AGE ARD (PRIMITIVE PLOUGH)

Alwyn S. Evans

fig.19

162

and the Roman period, more advanced ploughs were in use. These were confined to the continental mainland and southern Britain. They had a metal blade and could dig a satisfactory furrow. (Fig. 19)

It is fairly certain however, that on the hills behind Penmaenmawr society was not sophisticated and its technology not very advanced. It might be safer to assume that although field systems in the vicinity might imply that they had ploughs, at best they would have been of the more basic design. Perhaps they used digging sticks and hand held draw poles.

If they did use a simple form of ox or woman drawn plough like the ard it is not unlikely that the soldiers from Caerhun or Caernarfon would have told them of improvements they had seen both further south and in other lands. These improvements could have been undertaken with the aid of the garrison blacksmiths or farriers. This should not be seen as benevolence on the part of the garrison troops: a proportion of their food was grown locally as a form of tax. It was in their interest to encourage improved production!

Whatever their method, the villagers appeared to have been fairly successful farmers. We know that several households had querns for grinding corn. It's obvious therefore that they were able to store seed corn for annual use otherwise they would not have had crops from year to year. If we accept that they stayed in the fortified village over winter and did that for two or three hundred winters then we should assume that they had the food to sustain themselves and that as well as seed corn they had a corn surplus and were able to store it.

The sometimes accepted method of digging a storage pit in which to store grain does not appear to have been practised here: the ground was undoubtedly too hard and rocky.

Although storing corn in a damp hole in the ground does not seem like a good idea, it apparently worked quite well A hole was dug some six feet deep and varying in diameter according to need and ease of excavation. It narrowed toward the top to form a bell shape. The sides and bottom were lined with clay or stone. (Fig. 20) A fire was then lit in the hole in order to harden the clay, the fire was cleared out afterwards and the corn was stored within. The top was then covered with a flat stone or something similar and sealed with clay. The seeds on the surface and those nearest the clay or soil would germinate. During the process of germination they used up the oxygen and released carbon Di-oxide, this served to preserve the bulk of the corn or wheat until the seal was broken again. Once the seal was broken then all the remaining grain had to be decanted into smaller vessels to be used up fairly rapidly.

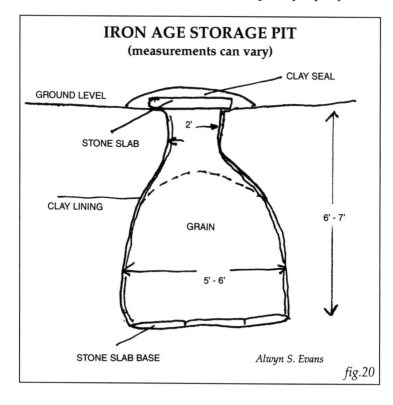

IRON AGE STORAGE PIT
(measurements can vary)

CLAY SEAL

GROUND LEVEL

2'

STONE SLAB

CLAY LINING

GRAIN

6' - 7'

5' - 6'

STONE SLAB BASE

Alwyn S. Evans

fig.20

Some of the huts on the mountainside were considerably smaller than the others and did not appear to have been lived in. were they used to store corn? The Roman amphorae would have been ideal for the purpose.

We know that the basic fare was likely to have been a vegetable based gruel, boosted from time to time, if the hunt was successful, by meat or fish.

Fish traps

From time to time fish traps of uncertain age have been uncovered on the beach. Although of medieval and later date the basic principle used in these traps is very similar to those in earlier traps found on waterside Iron Age sites. It seems highly likely that fish featured in the villagers' diet. It was available both from the sea and from the streams on the hills. Until the latter half of the twentieth century mackerel and herring were to be found in great quantities in the coastal waters of North Wales. Shells taken from the debris found in some of the huts point to the likelihood of seafood other than fish being utilised as well.

By this time, contact with the Roman garrisons would have meant better quality pottery able to resist direct heat and, as a result, perhaps hotter meals.

The Romans took their food rather seriously and might have been willing to pass on their secrets about such things as fish pastes and spicy herbs, if only to show their superiority. Unearthed evidence has identified other sources of nourishment. Identified bones let us know that they ate their oxen and pigs when they could no longer feed them and, when desperate, even their horses.

Cannibalism?

Human bones discovered recently in a Gloucester cave showed evidence of cannibalism. A thighbone had been carefully split lengthways, something that cannot happen accidentally, and the marrow scraped out. Many of the bones showed scrape marks which suggested that they had been cleaned by tools and not gnawed by teeth. The bones, believed to be those of at least seven Celtic tribesmen, were radiocarbon dated to between 30 BC and 130 AD. One archaeologist at the site suggested that the victims could well have been the elderly, the sick or criminals.

No suggestion of such activity was ever discovered at Pen-y-Dinas where all bones found were identified as being those of animals but it does give an idea of the desperation that must have been felt by some communities during periods of famine: perhaps brought on by extreme weather conditions or inter tribal war. The plight of the old and frail and the very young under such circumstances in a bleak spot like the elevated village in Penmaenmawr must have been horrendous. The survival rate of children born in such circumstances must have been low indeed.

Salting

In order to preserve it, meat was smoked or salted Some of the unoccupied huts could have been smokehouses, which might explain evidence of fires without sign of habitation The close proximity of the sea would have provided the resources for salting.

Discoveries made in other sites near the sea have revealed that large evaporation pans were fashioned, out of reach of the high tide and the water channelled into them .The contents were then allowed to evaporate. The resultant layer of crude salt and the underlying sand or mud was then dug out and roasted on fires until solid. The next step involved leaching out the salt by washing the mix with seawater, probably on some form of sieve. The liquid was then boiled to evaporation in bronze cauldrons and the resulting salt carried to the settlement. By doing this on a human chain system it is quite likely that a considerable amount of salt could be accumulated during the summer months for use in the winter. The production and sale or barter of salt could have been a trade by which a small team of men earned their living. There were such people as itinerant salt sellers in the Romano Celtic world. In Salzburg, which derived its name 'Salt town' from the commodity, salt was referred to as white gold. Salt was also used as payment for goods or labour hence the modern salary. The older word root Hal or Hall that appears in Germanic place names such as Halstatt also refers to salt. In Welsh, salt is halen and salty is hallt. A variation of Hal, Heli (To salt or to make salt) can be found in Pwllheli 'The salt pit or the salting pit' and Y Felin Heli 'The salt mill.' This occurrence of the same word root in south-eastern Germany and Austria and later in Wales is a sure indication of the steady spread of Celtic influence from east to west across Europe.

Today the hill slopes support bilberries, sloe berries, the odd wild strawberry clump, and crab apples. It is likely that similar fruits and possibly others, were here during the period of occupation of the hillfort. The women of the tribe particularly would have been aware of these and no doubt recognised wild herbs, which they would have used for flavouring food and possibly dressing wounds. We know that many of those herbs such as fat hen (Chenopodium Album) a type of wild spinach, were used both as flavouring and as a green vegetable which, when used in bulk was a good source of vitamin E. The villagers would undoubtedly have been aware of the beneficial results of eating such a vegetable but not of the reason why.

As was discussed earlier there is no evidence to prove that they possessed ploughs at all but even with the more basic tool they could have produced reasonably well tilled fields in which they could have grown a variety of pulses. Although we cannot be certain that the villagers used fish as a source of oil for cooking and lighting, the Romans did and the villager's contact with the garrisons might have seen that skill passed on. The lamps found confirm that oil of some kind was used.

One aspect of life in the village and the sources of sustenance that needs to be addressed, is the well. In a hilltop location within a construction which could be besieged water was a vital consideration.

In 1698 Edward Lhuyd makes reference to it thus 'Within the innermost (enclosure) there is a well giving water in the driest summer.' He makes no mention of the size or depth or of the structure. His claim that it gave water in the driest summer might suggest that he had made more than one trip to the top and on each occasion had seen it full. It hints too that he had made at least one of those ascents during a dry summer. Or was he simply generalising?

Between 1773 and 1776 Thomas Pennant had seen the spring on several occasions and he said that there 'is a well cut in the live rock' and that it was 'Supplied by the rains and kept full by the frequent impending vapours.' Although pennant does not give us any measurements, if he says it was cut in the live rock then would it be safe to assume that whoever cut it, if indeed it was cut, would not have gone to all that trouble to produce some insignificant hole in the ground. A spring, flowing constantly would certainly have kept a small well full but it would also have required an overflow. If, as Pennant says 'It was kept full' the resulting overflow would have created a small stream. No mention is made of such a stream.

Some twenty years after Pennant, Coleridge says that as they started to descend they accidentally turned over a large flat rock revealing a spring. Although it is difficult to see how one could *accidentally turn over a large stone* we must accept his version. He goes on to say that it hid a *little spring*, the waters of which 'became absorbed by the surface of the earth.' Was the well by then filled in and overgrown, allowing only a thin stream of water to penetrate to the surface?

Lytton, writing well into the following century tells us that 'The water bubbled from the *spring* that bubbled up everlastingly' and 'overflowed as from an artificial conduit.' He indicates then, however that it flowed between the wounded men in the camp. The camp was on the South-eastern side, the well to the West! Although some degree of poetic licence must be expected in a novel, it would be difficult to make a spring welling up on one side of a summit overflow down the opposite side. Lytton's account would be safer regarded as hearsay.

Are we to accept Pennant's version with its condensation and rain theory or do we accept that there was a spring? Others have ventured the same theory.

Mr Harold Hughes, a trained archaeologist and observer clearly calls it a well and does not elaborate. Surely if it were a spring would he not have said so? One could expect such a man to have been immediately inquisitive about the source of water in such a position.

In his presidential address to the Cambrian Archaeological Society in 1926 Willoughby Gardner Esq. FSA stated that, 'Water was obtainable at times near the summit but the main supply was from a spring outside the fortifications to the South.' The use of the term 'at times' suggests that he was of the opinion that the well did not have a permanent input. It is tempting to deduce from this that the well was indeed topped up by rain, mist and surface drainage.

From this I feel it would be safe to assume that the water for everyday use within the village would have been carried in on a daily basis and the well/spring reserved for emergency use. Willoughby Gardner's reference to 'A spring outside the defences to the south.' Is the only one I have been able to find which mentions such a source. Water would have been available from Yr Afon Ddu which rises to the south-west of Moelfre or from Afon Maes y Bryn a couple of hundred yards further on. These two and other tributaries combine to form the river that runs through Llanfairfechan. To the east, water is less easily available. Springs and rivulets occur amidst the quarry areas and Afon Gyrach (Afon y Wrach or Afon Nant y Wrach) is a mile or so to the east from where it runs down through the hamlet of Capelulo. Apart from this stream however, it would be difficult to prove the existence of any of the lesser sources nearly two thousand years ago. Many are in being today as the result of land drainage and quarrying activities.

Clothing

The number of spinning whorls found and their fairly even distribution shows that they were spinning something. It was almost certainly wool, sheep were herded in fairly large flocks which in times of danger and perhaps even at night, were herded together into the outer enclosure of the multivallate villages. They were kept for their wool and milk. Lacking the benefits of veterinarian attention, one third of lambs died in the first year and one half before eighteen months. This resulted in an almost permanent surfeit of milk. At the end of a useful life they were slaughtered for their meat, bones horns and skins.

The sheep of the time were of a long horned variety and differed from their modern counterparts in that they produced a wool that could be combed off rather than sheared. During the annual moult they were penned and combed with bone combs. The yarn produced was then used to weave or knit clothing.

The men wore a loose blouse and either a wrap similar to the original kilt or trousers or both. The trousers were held at the waist either by a cord or leather belt and secured again at the ankles. Interestingly there was a design in the material.

During the weaving process a chequered pattern similar to a modern Scottish plaid was formed. Shoes were made of leather, pulled up around the ankle. They were sometimes worn together with cloths used as ankle wraps similar to puttees.

Female clothing consisted of a long, perhaps shin or ankle length skirt and a blouse top that would have been quite recognisable today. I would consider capes or shawls to have been an outer coverall. Headgear was a variety of woollen or leather caps. It is likely that the wool was also used to make rough blankets for night and winter use. With the knowledge that we already have of other, similar sites of this period and the vital finds of the Harold Hughes excavation, we can see that it is possible to reconstruct a fairly accurate picture of life on the high moorland of ancient Penmaenmawr. Although they lived a life that was basic and rugged by today's standards they were not the cave dwellers of popular image. They even had religion although it should be pointed out that no obviously religiously connected artefacts were ever found at Pen-y-Dinas.

The early Celtic inhabitants of Britain worshipped many gods, and in some cases even shared the same gods with the Romans. Many were based on very ancient Greek and other Mediterranean deities that their ancestors had brought with them to Britain perhaps two thousand or more years earlier. I would hazard a guess that when these were worshipped it was in a collective, formal way, conducted by the tribal shaman or druid like figure. Others, and quite possibly those most commonly used, were local, personal and often connected with their daily lives. Known as a *Genius Loci*, 'spirit of the place' this kind of god or spirit needed no formal setting but could be invoked anywhere. Gods of water were popular, as were gods of the weather and the crops. Sulis was the main goddess of water, the corresponding Roman deity was Minerva the two grew together in Roman Britain to produce Sulis-Minerva, worshipped by conquered and conquerors alike. Taranis, the god of the sky was one of the main deities and has survived into modern times as the Welsh word for thunder, taran. Cernunnos, 'The Horned one' also remains with us as 'Cyrn,' horns in Welsh.

The oak tree was considered to have been of special significance. The druids revered it, especially when mistletoe grew on it. Nemeton was the name given to a sacred oak grove where religious gatherings were held. One wonders whether our villagers had their Nemeton amongst the oak covered slopes of Penmaenmawr. It is interesting to note that the habit of touching wood for luck is thought to have originated with the Celtic reverence of wood. A meeting under mistletoe had to be without arms and in good faith. Today's distorted version is a variant of the ancient.

Religion in the more advanced Celtic societies was organised and tended to take place within some type of enclosure: clearings in woods were popular. Perhaps our villagers used the long stones of the Druids' Circle. We cannot know, there is no means of telling. The lower reaches of Braich-y-Dinas were thickly covered by oak and other broad-leafed trees. Even the stretch of land which is pebble and sand today was covered with trees and shrub. According to one ancient chronicler, 'every March and June when ytt (*the sea*) ebbes farthest, are to be seene the rootes of greate oake and ashe att the furthest ebbe, . . . This I speake as an eye witness.'

Until the 1960's there were many more surviving patches of those old oaks to be seen on the slopes. The expanding quarry has swallowed most of them up. Coed Coch for instance no longer exists. Below the old 'Jolly' workings and in 'Coed Cwmlws' the descendants of those ancient stunted oaks still grow in the thin soil layer.

Unfortunately, the only relatively unbiased descriptions we have of the inhabitants of Britain, their habits, life styles and battle tactics, are those left to us by Ancient Greek travellers and merchants who had only limited contact with a small number of southern tribes. The historians and biographers who followed the Roman armies also left their impressions of the 'natives'. These 'War correspondents just as often compiled their accounts from comfortable quarters in the Mediterranean, relying solely on the information given to them by returning legions who were always alert to the opportunities for boosting their own reputations. These stories were undoubtedly coloured by the veterans' experiences and nearly always portrayed the opposition in a bad light. The reports we have are after all those of the winners. Although these histories are useful when attempting to reconstruct a Celtic scenario, it is vital that one is mindful of the exaggeration and bias in the Roman accounts.

It seems that the new technology that improved the lot of the southern, lowland tribes bypassed the hilltribes of the more remote highland regions, particularly those on the more northerly and westerly fringes. The resulting contrast in the standard of living could have been the catalyst for intertribal conflicts. If all the recognisable items of metal, glass or pottery discovered in the hillfort on Penmaenmawr were of Roman origin as the excavation reports imply, then a simple conclusion must be that the surviving indigenous items were all made of stone or clay. Perishable material like wood or cloth has naturally disappeared. The possible exceptions to this could have been the iron bars and even they are likely to have come to the settlement in the form of barter. At a time when the Iron Age was quite well established in most other western European areas, our villagers appear to have been still living in what was essentially an advanced Stone Age society. Having said that, I cannot believe that our villagers as a result of their obvious attempts at metalwork could not have produced some utensils, however crude.

Attacks

Another unanswered question surrounds Braich-y-Dinas. Unlike other strategically situated hill forts, especially in the South, there is no evidence to suggest that Rome ever attacked it. Why not? During his appraisal of the village, at least one historian has admitted surprise at this.

The settlement has, as has been seen in past accounts, been described as being lodging for twenty thousand men: of being able to withstand a legion, or of guarding the crossing to Anglesey and so on. If that were indeed the case, then surely it would have been a thorn in the flesh of those forces preparing to invade the island of Mona. Would the Romans have left this supposedly powerful hill fort occupying the high ground in their rear? It is inconceivable that any self-respecting Roman commander would have undertaken an invasion of the island while still having a substantial fortification on high ground immediately at his back. Study of Roman tactics implies that they would have either put the population to the sword or moved it to another location.

Could the truth be that when the Imperial armies sent detachments to reconnoitre the hill forts in the area and, if necessary, neutralise them: the reconnaissance parties found that Braich-y-Dinas, Tre'r Ceiri and others were so sparsely populated and their standard of existence so backward that they posed no threat? That might fit in with the paucity of Roman military accoutrements during the excavations. Certainly nothing has ever been found to indicate an assault. It should be remembered that Governor Pownall dismissed out of hand the idea that the village might ever have been a fort.

Let us consider another possibility. Was the camp already abandoned when the Romans arrived? Had its inhabitants evacuated and gone further West or over to the island, frightened of the impending attack? After their sack of the druidical centres on Anglesey, did the Romans forcibly resettle

174

a friendly tribe from another region? They were well known for their policy of 'divide and rule'.

In the event that the Romans found the inhabitants not to be a threat and left them where they were: imagine the spectacle that would have unfolded below them during the two invasions of Anglesey. In their elevated position they would have had a grandstand view. The first attack took place in 59/60 AD under Suetonius Paullinus who advanced from Wroxeter with X1V and part of the XX legions and their accompanying auxiliaries. The second happened some years later in 77/78 AD and was conducted by Julius Agricola. The occupants of Pen -y-Dinas would have seen the supply vessels as they rounded the Great Orme on their way from the temporary depot at Chester to resupply the Roman troops as they assembled on the Menai straits prior to the attacks on the druidical stronghold in 60 AD. They might even have heard the roar as the opponents clashed. The second campaign was conducted, according to Tacitus, to 'Contain an already beaten tribe.'

Goidelic influence

Migration of Goidelic tribes from Ireland to the whole of the West Coast of Wales had been going on for centuries. The word Goidel describes those Celtic tribes which had settled in Ireland and today the welsh word for the Irish is Gwyddelod. Many of the hutted encampments around the North Western and Southern coasts of Wales are known as 'Cytiau'r Gwyddelod,' the Irishmen's huts. There is one easily reached settlement on Holyhead Mountain where the huts are still in a fairly good condition. They resemble very closely those formerly on Braich-y-Dinas. Could it be that these Goidelic settlers took over the site in Penmaenmawr? There were periods when the garrisons in Britain were depleted as the result of emergencies in other parts of the empire. Could these moments of military weakness have been the opportunities for more aggressively inclined inroads by the Goidels?

A tenuous link with Ireland might possibly be construed from further addressing the name of the huge stone on the ridge running north west from Tal-y-Fan (Map ref. SH. 115. MR 742743). The stone, although broken and in several pieces is always referred to in the singular. It is called Maen Amor and the ridge, Cefn Maen Amor. In his 'Heart of Northern Wales,' Bezant Lowe suggests the possible translation to be a corruption of Cefn Maen Mawr giving Large Stone Ridge. This feels clumsy however as there is a definite A between the two consonants, N at the end of Maen and M in Amor. Even if we try the plural form of stone to give the extra syllable where the A in Amor has been excluded to form a possible Mawr; the plural of Maen is Meini and the name would become Cefn Meini Amor or, following Bezant Lowe's suggestion, Cefn Meini Mawr. In such a case I feel that the I in Meini would remain so and not become A even with corruption over time. I would prefer to stay with the current version.

Amor, sometimes Aamor, was a Celtic feminine first name. It is of Breton and Irish Gaelic origin rather than Brythonic and when used in Irish literature, appears as Aenor. Could this Aenor or Amor have been the wife, sister or daughter of a Goidelic chieftain on Braich-y-Dinas? Was she chieftain in her own right? It would not be unknown in Celtic society.

The areas of Demetia in the South West of Wales and the western edges of Gwynedd in the North were quite densely settled by the Goidels and they appear to have been left unmolested for a considerable time. In fact the kings of Demetia in South West Wales were of Goidelic lineage. In the North, tradition has it that the Llŷn peninsula is so named as a result of its occupation for so long by Goidels of the Laigin tribe who also gave their name to their Irish home, Leinster. Maybe they had come to some agreement with the Roman invader. Had they been left alone in their settlements on the understanding that they would act as a form of local militia?

Look-out posts

In the case of Braich-y-Dinas and Castell Caer Lleion on Conwy Mountain, could they have been utilised as look out posts for the fort at (Kanovium) Caerhun? The fort on Conwy Mountain or Mynydd y Dref is called Castell Caer Lleion. If we accept that as the correct name and not Castell Caer Seion as it is sometimes wrongly spelled on old maps, then we have another clue. Castell Caer Lleion translates as 'The castle of or belonging to, the fort of the legion.' (Lleng, Lleion and even Helen appear in place names throughout Wales to convey legionary influence) That could either be taken to mean the fort at Caerhun or the legionary fortress at Chester, known as Deva to the Romans and Caer Lleion to the Britons.

That name would not have been the original name for Conwy Mountain's fortification. It could only have been the name applied to the fortification by the local people *after* the coming of Rome when the use of the hilltop fort by Roman soldiers from Kanovium (Caerhun), or their local recruits, was established. I am not aware of an earlier name.

It is quite clear that the line of hilltop defences along the North Wales coast were built to defend against, or give warning of someone, but whom? Why is there no sign that they were ever attacked or slighted in any way in any kind of military confrontation? Were they built for protection from internecine warfare? Did local tribes build them against Irish invaders? Did Irish invaders build them against local tribes? Were some or all built or rebuilt at the instigation of Rome but not by Romans? From time to time it has been mooted whether buildings of a roughly rectangular shape found within the walls of the village could have indicated a Roman influence. It would be dangerous to accord any weight to such a suggestion as the huts could just as easily have been built as 'Hafotai', temporary summer shelters for shepherds; and at any time. Were they the first links in a long line of signal stations and horse depots, built to warn the legionary garrison at Chester of trouble brewing in the Irish Sea? If Goidels had already settled the area, perhaps the threat came not from Ireland but from another source. Mr Ivor Davies put forward an opinion that it could have come from the Isle of Man or even Scandinavia.

The hillforts become redundant

The fortified landing place for Roman naval vessels at Caergybi can be assigned to the re organisation of the forces in Britain under Count Theodosius, somewhere around 369/70 AD. Did the building of this small, but defended naval base with patrolling ships mean that the hillforts were made redundant? Smoke or fire signals might remain unseen during unfavourable weather. A messenger on foot or horseback on the other hand would be an unknown quantity A fast Roman ship, oar driven as well as sail, if unmolested could be in Chester, at the harbour on the Roodee with news of trouble, in quite a respectable time after leaving Holyhead.

End of an era

The fate of the villagers in Penmaenmawr as the imperial forces withdrew can only be guessed at. Did the village tribe fragment into small groups or even individual families which went their own way, leaving perhaps the die-hards to eke out a lonely existence on the mountain until the end finally came and the village was deserted?

There is little evidence to suggest that occupation of the

village on Braich-y-Dinas continued much, or indeed at all beyond the end of the fourth century AD. The decline seems to coincide with the lessening of Roman military intensity in the region. By the end of the fourth century, the Roman Garrisons in Britain were closing down and pulling out; handing over the responsibility of defence to locally recruited but probably roman trained militia. Could it be that the hill forts were becoming surplus to requirements? Did peace or disorder come to the coastal area as the military presence declined? Were the young men tempted by the life of a Roman auxiliary soldier? Regular money, food and excitement must have been pretty strong incentives for a youngster bored with sheep herding and the Spartan conditions on a bleak hillside.

When Magnus Maximus (The Macsen Wledig of Welsh literature) denuded Wales of its military protection in 383 AD. in order to go to Gaul to stake his claim as emperor in the West, did recruits from Braich-y-Dinas go with him? It is possible. Soldiers described as *Seguntiensis*, that is, British soldiers from the former garrison at Caernarfon were recorded as having been part of the 'Auxilia Palantina' operating under the COMES ILLYRICI in ILLYRICUM. That equates with modern Southeast Austria and the Dalmatian coast of Yugoslavia. It is unlikely they would have returned to Britain after experiencing such a place. If they survived their military service, auxiliaries, who were then awarded Roman citizenship tended to settle where their service came to an end.

Undoubtedly there will be other theories put forward, some will make sense while others will be wildly speculative. One of them might even be the right one. The thing is that we will never know. The people have gone, the fort has gone and now even the mountaintop has gone, blown into oblivion. There is nothing left to tell us what might have been in those far off troubled times.

Afterwards

The story of Braich-y-Dinas is not quite finished. Before the official excavation, finds had been made on the surface from time to time: they were accidental, not the result of determined searches. After the eventual destruction, evidence continued to come to light. Some casual finds were made and are still made by walkers but most were as the result of the quarrying.

One of the earlier discoveries creates a few puzzling alternatives and deserves mention.

In the 1871 Archaeologia Cambrensis it was reported that a coin hoard came to light during quarrying operations just to the west of and above and behind the Pencoed crushing mill. There were about sixty coins, mostly 'Denarii' of good silver. Why a coin hoard? The odd coin is understandable, One reason and that most often suggested for a hoard to be buried is fear of imminent attack. As the hoard is of Roman coins then are we to believe that a Roman buried it? Why would any Roman have so much money on top of a mountain in a rather backward native village at a time of danger, and what would have been so menacing that he would feel the need to bury it?

The soldiers in the fort at Caerhun were not Roman Legionaries in the popular mould: they were auxiliaries. Soldiers recruited from conquered countries on the continent and the middle east and, later, from Britain. As auxiliaries they would receive about one third of the pay of a legionary soldier. A cache of sixty coins like that found at Penmaenmawr, of which most were Denarii, a fairly high denomination, could represent roughly two thirds of an ordinary auxiliary soldier's annual pay.

The Roman army encouraged saving and provided facilities such as strong rooms, pension funds and pay clerks within the fort for the safety of the individual soldier's pay. Why would he take it up a mountain? The picture of a Roman soldier burying his hard earned money and life savings on some remote Welsh hillside is romantic and would be easy to believe but there is one insurmountable problem. The difference in the dating of the coins: 101 years between the earliest and the latest minting. This dashes the lovely theory of the Roman soldier and impending doom and leads us to another, less colourful but more practical solution.

Could it then have been the private cache of the local chieftain? Something on those lines might make more sense. Was it the village's reward, paid over the years for undertaking Roman chores? If that were the case, then the 101 years between the latest possible issue of the first coin and the first issue of the latest would imply that over the years they hadn't received much for their trouble. From the later years of the second century AD, the actual content of the silver in the denarius declined. Was this buried loot the act of someone expecting hard times ahead? Possible, but doubtful. Is it likely that such a fiscal devaluation could be anticipated in such a remote outpost?

If the inhabitants of the village were moved as was suggested earlier, why was the hoard left behind? Did they have to leave with so little warning that there was no chance to recover it? What could have caused such a rapid evacuation? Perhaps the answer is more mundane. Did the owner die without revealing the hiding place? Did the owner go on a journey and not return? Was there unrest within the village? If so, the hoard might be a simple case of someone exercising prudence. The hiding of money in this way could suggest that there *was* a degree of tension on the hills, from whatever source, toward the end of the third century AD: a tension that made the owner or keeper of the little treasure anxious enough to bury it.

Another find made after the main 'dig' provokes some thought.

In January 1927, a looped and socketed bronze spearhead was found just outside the lower ramparts to the north of the summit cairn at approximately 1430ft. The object was badly damaged and the remaining part measured a little over 4 ins. long. It had apparently fallen with a small landslide of stones and earth during blasting operations on the 'Kimberly' bank. Mr Dunbavand the quarry foreman brought the find to the attention of Mr Ivor Davies who informed Mr Harold Hughes. What makes the weapon worth comment, apart from the fact that it is a spearhead, is its location when found and its age.

Its design and material place it as having been from the Bronze Age (Phase two) probably circa 1400 BC. That would put its manufacture at least 1450 to 1550 years before the accepted main occupation period of the village! Was it discarded by someone who occupied an earlier, smaller defensive work on the same site centuries earlier? If so, could that spearhead provide a link, admittedly a very weak link, with the people who erected Y Meini Hirion (Druids' Circle) so many years before? They were of the same period and they would have had weapons similar to this one. Did they use the pinnacle as a look out post or refuge before the coming of Rome and if so did they also have a small, defended shelter or compound there: the forerunner of the later village? Did they use the small plateau immediately to the east of the summit as a kind of annex to the main circle? It will be recalled that Pownall suggested just such a use in 1774 and so did the Honourable Society of Cymmrodorion just over a hundred years later in 1882.

On the other hand, it could just as easily have been found elsewhere, considered for repair and dumped there. Was it simply part of a collection of such bits waiting to be melted down to make domestic ware in the first or second century AD? Without knowing the circumstances under which it arrived on the summit, we must add the spearhead to the long list of tantalisingly loose ends. (Fig. 21)

In 1928, within one hundred feet of the benchmark for 1281 ft, a brooch was found. It was a fraction over three inches long and of Romano British style. (Fig. 22) A coin dated 139AD and

BRONZE SPEARHEAD FOUND ON SUMMIT

fig.21

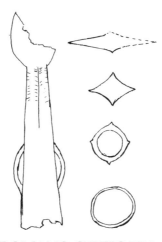

ROMANO CELTIC PIN
BACKWORTH TYPE I & II CENTURY A.D.
3″ (7 cm) long App. $1^1/4$″ (3 cm) high

fig.22

Alwyn S. Evans- AFTER W.F. GRIMES
Reproduced by kind permission of:
Royal Commission for Ancient and Historical Monuments Wales

from the reign of Antoninus Pius, was found with the brooch. Under normal circumstances the finding of such a coin with an artefact would have meant a solid dating guide. In this case the wide variance in the coin dates recovered from the area, even when found in groups, and the massive disturbance to the soil layers as a result of quarrying, meant that it would have been unwise to use the coin as the *sole* guide to when the brooch was made. Fortunately that was not necessary.

Dr W.F. Grimes described it as a 'perfect example of the Backworth Type. Typologically, it appears to be later than Backworth.'

The Backworth treasure came to light in the North of England in 1811 when a silver smith in Newcastle was sold an assortment of Roman finds. By the time of its acquisition by the British Museum in 1850, the bulk was almost completely dispersed. The site of the find was not known but if it were local to the north of England, and it probably was, then it's likely to have been on or near the course of Hadrian's Wall. Among the items were two quite large brooches which were coin dated to around 135 to 140 AD. It is these and their discovery in Backworth that gave the type its name. Grimes was therefore of the opinion that the brooch found on Braich-y-Dinas was made some time later than the second half of the second century. According to Dr Grimes, he was not aware of a *close* parallel to the Penmaenmawr brooch although a brooch of similar design was found in the Roman fort at Segontium (Caernarfon).

The Penmaenmawr brooch remained the property of Mr H.W.Darbishire of Tŷ Mawr. According to the museum at Cardiff the brooch is referred to as a Trumpet brooch, a common Roman brooch type from the middle of the 1st century AD. to the end of the 2nd century AD.

Further finds were made in 1932. Two coins were found after blasting, they were at 1500 ft, some ten to twenty feet apart. They were Roman but of a low denomination and very badly worn. One was about an inch in diameter and the other slightly larger. A head could be made out on the larger but beyond the fact that it was a head it was unrecognisable. That coin also had an inscription but it too was indecipherable. The coins remained the property of Mr H. Watkin Darbishire.

Also discovered, by separate quarrymen working in different places, was a variety of interesting stones. Two were quite large beach pebbles: one was nine inches long by nearly five and a half inches across and three and three quarters thick. The second stone was a piece that had been broken from a much larger original. The first was a pounder and one surface was clearly worn smooth where it had been held in the palm of a hand. The second was a polisher, the diameter was just short of three inches and the under surface was highly polished from years of domestic use.

Four smaller pebbles were also found, all their surfaces were highly polished. With these was an elongated stone some three and a quarter inches in length. It had squared sides with softly rounded edges and tapered slightly to one end: a Dr E. Greenly advised that it was an iron stone. At that time there were two iron stone quarries in Anglesey and others in the old counties of Denbighshire and Flintshire. After having seen the stone Dr Greenly was of the opinion that it was more likely to have been from the east rather than the Anglesey quarries. He does not appear to have given an explanation for his decision. The conditions under which the stones were discovered meant that their positions when found were not recorded.

1934 brought to light more historical gems. Quarrying was slowly but surely eating away at the summit and by then machinery was operating at an altitude of 1420 ft on the southern slope of the mountain. Again the articles fell down from what is known as the 'Overburden', that is the surface material, as the buckets tore at the mountain's heather covered hide. Once more the ever-vigilant Mr Dunbavand the quarry foreman was on the scene to retrieve and preserve. He was able to rescue a piece of metal that had obviously been worked and had the appearance of having been a retaining rim of some description. After the initial find, Mr Dunbavand spent many hours searching the area for any other bits and pieces but to no avail. This search was very necessary from an archaeological viewpoint but must have been a forlorn and presumably dangerous task as earth and rock were being removed from the spot with an electric shovel capable of lifting four cubic yards at a time.

This use of 'quarry' time to search showed an extremely benevolent and far seeing attitude on the part of the quarry owners and staff: those were still the days of extremely strict working conditions with little time or sympathy for 'distractions'. Despite Mr Dunbavand's best efforts we can only imagine what must have been lost as the machinery tore at the gorse and heather.

The article, which turned out to be part of a mount from the rim of a tankard, was taken to Mr H. Watkin Darbishire who as usual passed it on to Mr Ivor E Davies for onward transport to Mr Harold Hughes for identification. It was part of a drinking tankard.

The mount was four and a half inches long and made of bronze. It was slightly curved and would have formed an internal diameter of five and five eighths inches. It had seven lobes suspended on the underside. The centre lobe was considerably bigger than the others with a hole in its centre. Four of the other lobes were also pierced but had rivets through them which appeared to have been dummies. It seems they were decoration only and were never meant to have secured the mount to wooden staves, which made up the vessel. The rivet in the outer hole retained its shank. The rivet was missing from the sixth lobe. It was thought that the outer rivets held the rim in place while the others were for decoration only. The large lobe had a flat even recess running horizontally across it, which could have been meant as a securing point for a handle.

It was thought that two rivets would have secured the handle, one at the top and the other at the bottom, which went through the bronze and the wooden staves.

Was it once someone's pride and joy perhaps even a sign of someone's status? No decision appears to have been reached as to whether it was locally constructed or imported. The latter is probably more likely. Another, more complete tankard of similar date and format had been found at Trawsfynydd. With this as a guide, the remnants found at Braich-y-Dinas could be reconstructed. (Fig. 23)

The other finds were a saddle quern and a spindle whorl, both of the same design, period and general condition as those found during the main excavations. They were both turned up at about 1400ft. Although any find carries with it some excitement, the stone implements were by now rather run of the mill.

No doubt further finds will be made as people roam over the moors. It is to be hoped that such finds would be publicised so that further pieces, however small, can be added to the

TANKARD RIM FOUND ON PEN-Y-DINAS

fig.23

Crown Copyright: Royal Commission for Ancient and Historical Monuments Wales

Alwyn S. Evans - AFTER W. ASPDEN 1934

jigsaw of life in ancient Penmaenmawr. Perhaps then people might realise that those bits of faintly interestingly shaped stones or metal that now and then turn up were once the household possessions of a people who lived their lives on our mountain two thousand years ago.

List of coins found during excavations on Pen-y-Dinas

1911-1912	nil
1912-1913	nil
1921-1922	nil
1922-1923	Denarius of Trajan
	Denarius of Hadrian
	Denarius of Nerva
	Denarius illegible
	Denarius, very good condition, Nerva 97 AD
	Denarius, worn Trajan 112-117 AD
	Denarius, very worn, Hadrian 118 AD
	Denarius, very worn and broken

Acknowledgements

I would like to take this opportunity to thank all the organisations listed below and the individuals within them who have shown extreme patience with a total amateur. All have been unstinting in their generous provision of material and advice. Their guidance and kindness is much appreciated.

The National Library of Wales Aberystwyth
The Royal Commission for the Ancient and Historical Monuments, Wales. Aberystwyth
National Museum and Galleries of Wales Collections Centre, Department of Industry, Nant Garw
Sites and Monuments Records Office, Gwynedd Archaeological Trust, Bangor
The Gwynedd Archive Services, Caernarfon
University of Cambridge, Committee for Aerial Photography
Chester City Council
Grosvenor Museum Chester
Buxton Museum
Manchester University
Archaeologia Cambrensis
Liverpool University
Llandudno Library
Forestry Enterprises, Llanrwst
Department of History and Welsh History, University of Wales, Bangor
Countryside Council for Wales, Bangor
Bangor Museum
Mrs. Frances Llywelyn, Bangor

Bibliography

Archaeologia Cambrensis, Excavation Reports, Pen-y-Dinas, 1912, 1913, 1915, 1922, 1923, 1928.

Berresfod Ellis, Peter, *The Celtic Empire*, Constable and Company Ltd., 1991.

— *Caesar's Invasion of Britain*, Orbis Publishing, 1978.

Bingley AM, The Rev. W., *North Wales during summer of 1798-1801*, Cambrian Traveller's Guide, 2nd edition, 1813.

Briard, Jacques, *The Bronze Age in Barbarian Europe*, Routledge Keegan and Paul, 1976.

Brockhampton Reference, *The Dictionary of the Celts*, Brockhampton Press, 1997.

Burl, Aubrey, *Rings of Stone*, pp. 182/3, Frances Lincoln Ltd., 1979

— *Prehistoric Avebury*, Yale University Press, 1979.

— *The Stonehenge people*, J.M. Dent, 1987.

Caernarvonshire Historical Society Transactions, No. 35, 1974; No. 59, 1998.

Cambrian Traveller's Guide, 2nd edition, 1813.

Chadwick, Nora, *The Celts*, Pelican Books, 1977.

Cunliffe, Prof. Barry, *Danebury, Anatomy of an Iron Age hillfort*, B.T.Batsford Ltd., London, 1983

— *The Ancient Celts*, Oxford University Press. 1997.

Delaney, Frank, *Legends of the Celts*, Hodder and Stoughton, 1989; Grafton 1991

— *The Celts*, Grafton, 1989.

Dyer, James, *Hillforts of England and Wales*, Shire Publications, 1981.

Glob, P.V., *The Mound People, (Danish Bronze Age Man preserved)*, Faber and Faber, 1974.

Green, Amanda J., *Exploring the World of the Druids*, Thames and Hudson, 1997.

Hazzeldine Warren, S., 'A Kind of Sheffield of the Stone Age',

Excavations of a Neolithic Axe Factory on the Graiglwyd, Penmaenmawr 1919-1921.

Johns, Catherine, *The Jewellery of Roman Britain*, Celtic and Classical Traditions, University of Michigan Press, University of London Press, 1996.

Johnson, Steven, *Later Roman Britain*, Routledge and Keegan Paul, 1980.

Kendall MA, The Rev. H.G.O., *Further Excavations at the Graiglwyd, Penmaenmawr Neolithic Axe Factory Penmaenmawr*, 1926.

Keppie, Lawrence, *The making of The Roman Army from Republic to Empire*, B.T. Batsford Ltd., 1987.

Laing, Lloyd, *Celtic Britain*, Routledge Keegan and Paul, 1979.

Lynch, Frances, *Prehistoric Anglesey*, Anglesey Antiquarian Society, Revised Edition, 1991.

Mac Cana, Proinsias, *Celtic Mythology*, Hamlyn, 1983.

McGrail, Sean, *Ancient Boats*, Shire Publications, 1983.

Myvyrian Archaiology of Wales, Collected from Ancient manuscripts, Volume 1, Poetry 1801.

Nash-Williams, V.E., *The Roman Frontier in Wales*, 2nd edition, University of Wales Press, 1969.

Pearson, Michael Parker, *Bronze Age Britain*, B.T. Batsford, 1993.

Peddie, John, *Invasion – The Roman Conquest of Britain*, Alan Sutton Publishing Ltd., 1987.

Piggot, Stuart, *The Druids*, Penguin, 1977.

Ross, Anne, *Everyday Life of the Pagan Celts*, Carousel, 1972.

Sharkey, John, *Celtic Mysteries, The Ancient Religion*, Thames and Hudson, 1979.

Sorrel, Alan, *Reconstructing the Past*, Batsford Academic & Educational Ltd., 1981.

Wacher, John, *The Coming of Rome*, Routledge and Keegan Paul, 1979.

Walkley, Victor, *Celtic Daily Life*, Robinson Publishing, 1997.

Webster, Graham, *Rome Against Caratacus, The Roman campaigns in Britain AD48-58*, B.T. Batsford, 1981.

— *The Roman Imperial Army of the first and second century AD*, 3rd edition, A. and C. Black Ltd., 1985.

— *The Roman Invasion of Britain*, Batsford Academic and Educational Ltd., 1981.

Y Cymmrodor, Transactions of the Honourable Society of Cymmrodorion of London, Vol. V, 1882.

This Bibliography is representative and does not include many other books, a multitude of documents, maps, pictures, etc. used during the compilation of this history,